A GUIDE TO

PYGMALION

MARY HARTLEY

WITH TONY BUZAN

Hodder & Stoughton

Cover photograph ©: Leslie Howard and Wendy Hiller, The Ronald Grant Archive
Mind Maps: Ann Jones
Illustrations: Karen Donnelly

ISBN 0 340 75320 X

First published 1999
Impression number   10 9 8 7 6 5 4 3 2 1
Year   2002 2001 2000 1999

The 'Teach Yourself' name and logo are registered trade marks of
Hodder & Stoughton Ltd.

Typeset by Transet Limited, Coventry, England.
Printed in Great Britain for Hodder & Stoughton Educational, a division of
Hodder Headline Plc, 338 Euston Road, London NW1 3BH by Cox and Wyman Ltd,
Reading, Berks.

CONTENTS

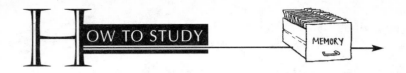

There are five important things you must know about your brain and memory to revolutionize the way you study:

◆ how your memory
   ('recall') works *while* you are learning
◆ how your memory works *after* you have finished learning
◆ how to use Mind Maps – a special technique for helping you with all aspects of your studies
◆ how to increase your reading speed
◆ how to prepare for tests and exams.

Recall during learning
– THE NEED FOR BREAKS

When you are studying, your memory can concentrate, understand and remember well for between 20 and 45 minutes at a time. Then it needs a break. If you carry on for longer than this without a break your memory starts to break down. If you study for hours non-stop, you will remember only a small fraction of what you have been trying to learn, and you will have wasted hours of valuable time.

So, ideally, *study for less than an hour*, then take a five to ten minute break. During the break listen to music, go for a walk, do some exercise, or just daydream. (Daydreaming is a necessary brain-power booster – geniuses do it regularly.) During the break your brain will be sorting out what it has been learning, and you will go back to your books with the new information safely stored and organized in your memory banks. We recommend breaks at regular intervals as you work through the Literature Guides. Make sure you take them!

Recall after learning
– THE WAVES OF YOUR MEMORY

What do you think begins to happen to your
memory straight after you have finished learning something?
Does it immediately start forgetting? No! Your brain actually
increases its power and carries on remembering. For a short
time after your study session, your brain integrates the
information, making a more complete picture of everything it
has just learnt. Only then does the rapid decline in memory
begin, and as much as 80 per cent of what you have learnt can
be forgotten in a day.

However, if you catch the top of the wave of your memory,
and briefly review (look back over) what you have been
studying at the correct time, the memory is stamped in far more
strongly, and stays at the crest of the wave for a much longer
time. To maximize your brain's power to remember, take a few
minutes and use a Mind Map to review what you have learnt
at the end of a day. Then review it at the end of a week, again
at the end of a month, and finally a week before your test or
exam. That way you'll ride your memory
wave all the way there – and beyond!

The Mind Map ®
– A PICTURE OF THE WAY YOU THINK

Do you like taking notes? More importantly, do you like having to
go back over and learn them before tests or exams? Most
students I know certainly do not! And how do you take your
notes? Most people take notes on lined paper, using blue or
black ink. The result, visually, is boring! And what does *your*
brain do when it is bored? It turns off, tunes out, and goes to
sleep! Add a dash of colour, rhythm, imagination, and the whole
note-taking process becomes much more fun, uses more of your
brain's abilities, and improves your recall and understanding.

A Mind Map mirrors the way your brain works. It can be used
for note-taking from books or in class, for reviewing what you
have just studied, and for essay planning for coursework and
in tests or exams. It uses all your memory's natural techniques
to build up your rapidly growing 'memory muscle'.

You will find Mind Maps throughout this book. Study them, add some colour, personalize them, and then have a go at drawing your own – you'll remember them far better! Stick them in your files and on your walls for a quick-and-easy review of the topic.

HOW TO DRAW A MIND MAP

1 Start in the middle of the page. This gives your brain the maximum room for its thoughts.
2 Always start by drawing a small picture or symbol. Why? Because a picture is worth a thousand words to your brain. And try to use at least three colours, as colour helps your memory even more.
3 Let your thoughts flow, and write or draw your ideas on coloured branching lines connected to your central image. These key symbols and words are the headings for your topic. Start like the Mind Map on page 13.
4 Then add facts and ideas by drawing more, smaller, branches on to the appropriate main branches, just like a tree.
5 Always print your word clearly on its line. Use only one word per line.
6 To link ideas and thoughts on different branches, use arrows, colours, underlining, and boxes (see page 20).

HOW TO READ A MIND MAP

1 Begin in the centre, the focus of your topic.
2 The words/images attached to the centre are like chapter headings; read them next.
3 Always read out from the centre, in every direction (even on the left-hand side, where you will have to read from right to left, instead of the usual left to right).

USING MIND MAPS

Mind Maps are a versatile tool – use them for taking notes in class or from books, for solving problems, for brainstorming with friends, and for reviewing and working for tests or exams – their uses are endless! You will find them invaluable for planning essays for coursework and exams. Number your main branches in the order in which you want to use them and off you go – the main headings for your essay are done and all your ideas are logically organized!

Super speed reading

It seems incredible, but it's been proved – the faster you read, the more you understand and remember! So here are some tips to help you to practise reading faster – you'll cover the ground more quickly, remember more, and have more time left for both work and play.

◆ First read the whole text (whether it's a lengthy book or an exam or test paper) very quickly, to give your brain an overall idea of what's ahead and get it working. (It's like sending out a scout to look at the territory you have to cover – it's much easier when you know what to expect!) Then read the text again for more detailed information.

◆ Have the text a reasonable distance away from your eyes. In this way your eye/brain system will be able to see more at a glance, and will naturally begin to read faster.

◆ Take in groups of words at a time. Rather than reading 'slowly and carefully' read faster, more enthusiastically.

◆ Take in phrases rather than single words while you read.

◆ Use a guide. Your eyes are designed to follow movement, so a thin pencil underneath the lines you are reading, moved smoothly along, will 'pull' your eyes to faster speeds.

Preparing for tests and exams

◆ Review your work systematically. Cram at the start of your course, not the end, and avoid 'exam panic'!

◆ Use Mind Maps throughout your course, and build a Master Mind Map for each subject – a giant Mind Map that summarizes everything you know about the subject.

◆ Use memory techniques such as mnemonics (verses or systems for remembering things like dates and events).

◆ Get together with one or two friends to study, compare Mind Maps, and discuss topics.

AND FINALLY...

Have *fun* while you learn – it has been shown that students who make their studies enjoyable understand and remember everything better and get the highest grades. I wish you and your brain every success! (Tony Buzan)

HOW TO USE THIS GUIDE

This guide assumes that you have already read *Pygmalion*, although you could read 'Background' and 'The story of *Pygmalion*' before that. It is best to use this guide alongside the play. You could read 'Who's Who?' and 'Themes' without referring to the play, but you will get more out of these sections if you do refer to it to check the points made in these sections, and especially when tackling the questions designed to test your recall and help you to think about the play.

The 'Commentary' section can be used in a number of ways. One way is to read a scene or part of a scene in the play, and then read the commentary for that section. Keep on until you come to a test section, test yourself – then have a break! Alternatively, read the Commentary for a scene or part of a scene, then read that scene in the play, then go back to the Commentary. Find out what works best for you.

'Topics for discussion and brainstorming' gives topics that could well feature in exams or provide the basis for coursework. It would be particularly useful for you to discuss them with friends, or brainstorm them using Mind Map techniques (see p. vi).

'The exam essay' is a useful 'night before' reminder of how to tackle exam questions, and 'Model answer' gives an example of an A-grade essay and the Mind Map and plan used to write it.

The questions

Whenever you come across a question in the guide with a star ✪ in front of it, think about it for a moment. You could even jot down a few words in rough to focus your mind. There is not usually a 'right' answer to these questions: it is important for you to develop your own opinions if you want to get an 'A'. The 'Test yourself' sections are designed to take you about 10–20 minutes each – which will be time well spent. Take a short break after each one.

Page numbers

Page numbers refer to the Longman Literature edition. If you have another edition, the page numbers may be different, although the Act numbers will be the same.

KEY TO ICONS

Themes

A **theme** is an idea explored by an author. Whenever a theme is dealt with in the guide, the appropriate icon is used. This means you can find where a theme is mentioned just by flicking through the book. Go on – try it now!

Language

Class

Money

Education

Women

STYLE AND LANGUAGE

This heading and icon are used in the Commentary wherever there is a special section on the author's choice of words and imagery.

The author

George Bernard Shaw was a major influence on drama at the beginning of the twentieth century. He was an outspoken, controversial figure who shocked and entertained the Victorian and Edwardian public with his wit and his social criticism. Throughout his life he was an energetic dramatist, journalist and critic who expressed his passion for equality and his dislike of pomposity and prejudice through his numerous speeches and writings. Shaw died at the age of 93, still writing and planning his next play.

AS A BOY

Shaw was born in Ireland in 1856. His father was a civil servant and a merchant; he was also a heavy drinker. Shaw's mother was a music teacher who passed on her love of music to her son. She herself was taught to sing by a great musician who lived in their household, and followed this man to London, leaving Shaw behind. One biographer, Peter Ackroyd, suggests that Shaw was very hurt by his mother's departure, and that he wrote *Pygmalion* after her death to rewrite his past by creating a professional relationship between a pupil and a teacher.

HIS LIFE'S WORK

After leaving school, which he hated, Shaw became a clerk for five years, then joined his mother in London in 1876. This was the start of his writing career. Shaw became interested in politics and social reform, and emerged as a critic of music, art and literature as well as an acclaimed playwright. In 1926 he received the Nobel Prize for literature. With typical wit, Shaw said that a grateful public awarded him this prize because he had not published anything during that year.

Shaw wrote over 50 plays and countless pamphlets on political and economic subjects, not to mention thousands of letters. In his writing and speeches he presented his opinions on subjects ranging from his belief in vegetarianism and teetotalism to his ideas about how the country should be run.

A LIGHT GOES OUT

When this great public figure died in 1950, theatres observed a two-minute silence and the lights of Broadway were switched off as a token of respect.

SHAW AND DRAMA

Shaw's plays deal with controversial and uncomfortable issues. His first play, *Widowers' Houses*, attacks the evils of slum landlordism, and although the play was not a box-office success, Shaw was delighted with the sensation created by its daring theme. Another play, *Mrs Warren's Profession*, deals with the economic causes of prostitution, and caused a similar sensation with audiences in Britain and America.

Shaw felt that plays should be concerned with ideas and social and moral issues, and that they should teach us something. Each of his plays begins with a Preface in which Shaw discusses the play's themes and his aims in writing it. Some of the Prefaces are as long as the plays themselves!

PYGMALION

Pygmalion was an instant hit with the public when it was first staged in London in 1914. It was turned into a film in 1938, and in 1956 it was adapted as a stage musical, *My Fair Lady*. Shaw wrote the part of Eliza for the actress Mrs Patrick Campbell, with whom he fell in love. He was devastated when she disappeared in the middle of final rehearsals – to get married.

THE MYTH OF PYGMALION

Pygmalion is based on a Greek myth. (Myths are stories, usually involving gods and humans, which often contain hidden meaning.) Pygmalion was a sculptor who was devoted to the beautiful statues he created. One particular statue, carved out of ivory, was so beautiful that Pygmalion fell in love with it. He prayed to the goddess Aphrodite to make the statue come to life. Aphrodite granted his prayer, and the statue became a beautiful woman, named Galatea. Pygmalion married his creation. ✪ As you read Shaw's play, think about its similarities to, and differences from, the myth.

SHAW AND LANGUAGE

Throughout his life Shaw campaigned for a change in the English spelling system, and in his will he left a large amount of money to be spent on rewriting great literary works in a different alphabet so that people would be able to read them more easily. In *Pygmalion* we see his interest in the way people react to 'bad' language, and their different attitudes to its use by particular classes. In the play Shaw also presents his convictions that people should not be limited by the way they speak, nor judged and defined by their accents and grammar.

SHAW AND POLITICS

Shaw was a prominent member of the Fabian Society, a socialist group formed in 1884. This was not a revolutionary group, but one which aimed for social change through education and argument. Shaw's desire for a more just and equal society is seen in his energetic commitment to the society's aims.

HISTORICAL BACKGROUND

A few months after the first performance of *Pygmalion* in 1914, the First World War began. It continued until 1918. The years leading up to the war saw the beginnings of social change as measures such as school meals and old age pensions were introduced to help the poorer classes. The workforce became more educated and more organized, and were less willing to accept a lower position in society. However, reforms that benefited the working class met stiff opposition, and thousands of people continued to suffer deprivation and hardship. Reform was slow in a country facing industrial problems, such as violent strikes by workers in 1911 and 1912, unrest from the Suffragette movement, and growing tension in Europe. The division between social classes remained strong.

3

THE *SUFFRAGETTE* MOVEMENT

Suffragettes campaigned, sometimes violently, for votes for
women. Before 1918 women under the age of 30 could not
vote, and before 1928 women could not vote until they were
21. Women demonstrating for the right to vote clashed with
the police and many were arrested. Some women went on
hunger strike and were forcibly fed. Shaw supported women's
suffrage and made speeches and wrote letters to newspapers
attacking the government's legislation. He said that women
should *shoot, kick, maim, destroy* until they won the vote.
✪ How does *Pygmalion* deal with the subject of women's
equality? Think about this question as you read the play.

LONDON THEATRE

Very popular at this time were 'girl musicals', often staged at
the Gaiety Theatre. These plays told rags-to-riches stories,
usually about young poor women who married into the
aristocracy. A wedding at the end was obligatory. *Pygmalion*
was a huge success although Shaw refused to indulge the
popular taste for a Cinderella-type heroine and a romantic
happy ending. ✪ How is Eliza different from a meek, helpless
woman who needs a man to rescue her?

Shaw admired the work of Henrik Ibsen, a Norwegian
dramatist whose plays were different from romantic and
melodramatic works that were popular at the time. Like Ibsen,
Shaw stressed the importance of thought and intelligence, and
was interested in how characters react to social forces and
relate to each other. Other playwrights producing dramas to do
with ideas were J. M. Barrie and John Galsworthy.

THE STORY OF PYGMALION

Act 1

SHELTERING

A group of people shelter from the rain under the front of a church in the **Covent Garden** market. Among them is an upper-middle-class family, the **Eynsford Hills**, who have been to the **theatre**. The son, **Freddy**, has been trying to find a **cab** to take his mother and **sister** home. Returning with no success, Freddy is sent off again, and bumps into a **girl** selling **flowers**.

NOTE-TAKING

Eliza, the flower girl, tries to persuade an elderly **military** gentleman to buy some flowers. One of the people sheltering warns her that someone is **taking notes** on what she says. Eliza is scared that the man is writing down evidence to accuse her of being a prostitute. She protests that she is a **good girl**.

The note-taker is **Henry Higgins**, an expert in **phonetics**, who is making notes on the different **accents** and **dialects** he hears around him. He identifies the origins of individuals in the crowd from the way that they **speak**. The military gentleman is **Colonel Pickering**, also an expert in **language**, who has come to London to meet Professor Higgins. Higgins claims that he could teach Eliza to **speak like a duchess** in three months. The two men, delighted to have met each other, go off to have supper. Eliza goes home in a cab she can afford from the money that Higgins throws in her basket of flowers.

Act 2

AT HOME WITH HIGGINS

The next morning Higgins is showing Pickering his **laboratory**. **Eliza** turns up. She wants Higgins to teach her how to **speak differently** so that she can get a job in a **flower shop**. **Pickering** bets Higgins that he can't pass Eliza off as a duchess at the ambassador's garden party. Higgins accepts the challenge and tells his housekeeper, **Mrs Pearce**, to clean Eliza and dress her in different clothes. Mrs Pearce has to force Eliza into the **bath tub**. Mrs Pearce is **uneasy** about Higgins's plan for Eliza.

Eliza's **father**, a **dustman**, Alfred **Doolittle**, arrives. He hopes to get **money** from Higgins in exchange for his daughter. In the end he settles for **five pounds**. Higgins starts Eliza's **speech lessons**.

Act 3

AT HOME WITH MRS HIGGINS

Mrs Higgins is expecting guests on her at-home day. Henry has asked **Eliza** to attend to see if his mother's guests will think that she is a **lady**. The guests are the **Eynsford Hills**, the family who were waiting for a cab in **Covent Garden** at the beginning of the play. They do not recognize **Eliza** in her new role. Eliza's **accent** is perfect, but her **language** and **subject matter** are inappropriate. However, the guests believe that Eliza's way of speaking is the **height of fashion**. Freddy is **fascinated** by her. Afterwards, Mrs Higgins points out that Eliza is not yet ready to be presented in **high society**. Mrs Higgins also expresses concern for Eliza's future.

AT THE EMBASSY

Some time later, Eliza is taken for a **princess** at the embassy reception.

Act 4

WHAT ABOUT ME?

Higgins and **Pickering** are delighted with the success of the experiment. Eliza has been a great success at a **garden party**, a **dinner party** and the reception. Eliza is **angry** because her contribution has been ignored and, now that the experiment is over, her **future** is **uncertain**. Henry, however, cannot see the problem.

LOVE AND KISSES

Eliza leaves **Higgins**'s house. Outside she meets **Freddy**, who is in love with her and has been hanging around to be near her. They kiss and wander around the streets before getting a **cab**.

Act 5

A RESPECTABLE MAN

Higgins is **alarmed** to find Eliza gone, and informs the **police** of her disappearance. When he arrives at his **mother**'s house, he is astounded to discover that **Eliza** is upstairs. **Doolittle** arrives in a **wedding outfit**. As a result of Higgins telling a **wealthy American** about Doolittle's ideas on **morality**, the American has left Doolittle **money** on condition that he gives **lectures** on the subject. Doolittle has been forced to become respectable, and blames **Higgins** for this.

MARRYING FREDDY

Higgins tries to persuade **Eliza** to return to **his house**. He assures her that he treats everyone the same way, and says he misses her. Higgins suggests that **he**, **Eliza** and **Pickering** could live together as **equals**. Eliza **refuses** and says that she is going to marry **Freddy**. Eliza goes off with **Mrs Higgins** to her father's **wedding**.

SEQUEL

Eliza and Freddy marry and open a **shop**, which is eventually a success.

HOW MUCH CAN YOU REMEMBER?

Without looking back, try to fill in the blanks. You can use your own words as long as you keep the general sense.

Act 1

SHELTERING

A group of people shelter from the rain under the front of a church in the _____ _____ market. Among them is an upper-middle-class family, the _____ _____, who have been to the _____. The son, _____, has been trying to find a _____ to take his mother and _____ home. Returning with no success, Freddy is sent off again, and bumps into a _____ selling _____.

NOTE-TAKING

_____, the flower girl, tries to persuade an elderly _____ gentleman to buy some flowers. One of the people sheltering warns her that someone is _____ _____ on what she says. Eliza is scared that the man is writing down evidence to accuse her of being a prostitute. She protests that she is a

_____ _____.

The note-taker is _____ _____, an expert in _____, who is making notes on the different _____ and _____ he hears around him. He identifies the origins of individuals in the crowd from the way that they _____. The military gentleman is _____ _____, also an expert in _____, who has come to London to meet Professor Higgins. Higgins claims that he could teach Eliza to _____ _____ _____ _____ in three months. The two men, delighted to have met each other, go off to have supper. Eliza goes home in a cab she can afford with the money that Higgins throws in her basket of flowers.

Act 2

AT HOME WITH HIGGINS

The next morning Higgins is showing Pickering his _____.
_____ turns up. She wants Higgins to teach her how to

_____ _____ so that she can get a job in a _____
_____. _____ bets Higgins that he can't pass off Eliza as a
duchess at the ambassador's garden party. Higgins accepts the
challenge and tells his housekeeper, _____ _____, to clean
Eliza and dress her in different clothes. Mrs Pearce has to force
Eliza into the _____ _____. Mrs Pearce is _____ about
Higgins's plan for Eliza.

Eliza's _____, a _____, Alfred _____, arrives. He hopes
to get _____ from Higgins in exchange for his daughter. In
the end he settles for _____ _____. Higgins starts Eliza's
_____ _____.

Act 3

AT HOME WITH MRS HIGGINS

Mrs Higgins is expecting guests on her at-home day. Henry has
asked _____ to attend to see if his mother's guests will think
that she is a _____. The guests are the _____ _____, the
family who were waiting for a cab in _____ _____ at the
beginning of the play. They do not recognize _____ in her
new role. Eliza's _____ is perfect, but her _____ and
_____ _____ are inappropriate. However, the guests
believe that Eliza's way of speaking is the _____ _____
_____. Freddy is _____ by her. Afterwards, Mrs Higgins
points out that Eliza is not yet ready to be presented in
_____ _____. Mrs Higgins also expresses concern for
Eliza's _____.

AT THE EMBASSY

Some time later, Eliza is taken for a _____ at the embassy
reception.

Act 4

WHAT ABOUT ME?

_____ and _____ are delighted with the success of the
experiment. Eliza has been a great success at a _____
_____, a _____ _____ and the reception. Eliza is

The story of Pygmalion

Eliza is selling flowers in Covent Garden. Freddy knocks over her basket and his mother pays for the spoiled flowers

Eliza sells a flower to Colonel Pickering

Eliza is warned that a man (Higgins) is taking notes of everything she says

Higgins boasts that he could teach Eliza to speak like a duchess in three months. Higgins and Pickering meet

Eliza arrives at Higgins's house. She wants him to teach her to speak like a duchess

Pickering challenges Higgins to teach Eliza to speak like a duchess. Mrs Pearce gives Eliza a bath and new clothes

Eliza's father, Alfred Doolittle, arrives. He wants money in exchange for Eliza. Eliza's lessons begin

Eliza attends Mrs Higgins's at-home. The other guests are Freddy's family. Eliza uses some shocking language

Eliza is taken for a princess

Eliza is angry with Higgins and worried about her future now that the experiment is over

Eliza leaves the house and meets Freddy, who is in love with her

Higgins finds Eliza at his mother's house. Doolittle arrives. He is now wealthy and forced to be middle class

Higgins tries to persuade Eliza to return, but she says she is going to marry Freddy

Eliza and Mrs Higgins leave for Doolittle's wedding

_____ because her contribution has been ignored and, now that the experiment is over, her _____ is _____. Henry, however, cannot see the problem.

LOVE AND KISSES

Eliza leaves _____'s house. Outside she meets _____,who is in love with her and has been hanging around to be near her. They kiss and wander around the streets before getting a _____.

Act 5

A RESPECTABLE MAN

Higgins is _____ to find Eliza gone, and informs the _____ of her disappearance. When he arrives at his _____'s house, he is astounded to discover that _____ is upstairs. _____ arrives in a _____ _____. As a result of Higgins telling a _____ _____ about Doolittle's ideas on _____, the American has left Doolittle _____ on condition that he gives _____ on the subject. Doolittle has been forced to become respectable, and blames _____ for this.

MARRYING FREDDY

Higgins tries to persuade _____ to return to _____ _____. He assures her that he treats everyone the same way, and says that he misses her. Higgins suggests that _____, _____ and _____ could live together as _____. Eliza _____ and says that she is going to marry _____. Eliza goes off with _____ _____ to her father's _____.

SEQUEL

Eliza and Freddy marry and open a _____ which is eventually a _____.

Now you're clear about the plot, take a break before meeting a cast of characters.

WHO'S WHO?

The Mini Mind Map above summarizes the characters in *Pygmalion*. Test yourself by looking at the full Mind Map on p. 20, and then copying the Mini Mind Map and adding to it.

Henry Higgins

Henry Higgins is a vigorous, dynamic character, full of contradictions, who dominates the play just as he dominates the people around him. He is often unreasonable and infuriating, but Shaw tells us that he is *likeable even in least reasonable moments* (Act 2). ✪ As you read the play, think about Higgins's good and bad points, and to what extent you like and admire him in the end. You could begin a Mind Map of your observations of the 'plus and minus' sides of Higgins's character as you read the play.

AN EXPERT

Professor Higgins is an expert in the field of phonetics, universally admired for his professional knowledge and experience. He is proud of his reputation and guards it jealously. He hates the idea of Eliza becoming a teacher of phonetics, particularly when she says that she will assist Higgins's former pupil, Nepommuck. With typical vehemence, Higgins says he will wring her neck if she passes on his methods and discoveries to that *imposter*.

13

Higgins's interest in language has become an obsession, and he pursues his own aims without considering other people's feelings. He is in his element when we first see him, absorbed in taking notes on the way Eliza and the people in the crowd speak. Higgins enjoys showing off to the crowd, and commands the centre of attention through his brilliance and showmanship. ❂ Where and how would a present-day Higgins demonstrate his cleverness? Writing books? Giving lectures? Anything else? His treatment of Eliza demonstrates his thoughtlessness and insensitivity. In his enthusiasm for the experiment, Higgins ignores Eliza's feelings and cannot see that her life has been irrevocably changed. He is so focused on his work that even when Eliza tells him that she wouldn't marry him if he asked, he corrects her grammar: *Than he is; not 'than what he is'* (Act 5).

Not only is Higgins an expert in other people's use of language, but he also displays an impressive command of rhetoric (the art of using language eloquently, for effect). A good example is his speech in Act 2 beginning *There! That's all you'll get out of Eliza*, where we see Higgins carried away by the force and flow of his exuberant language. His venomous attack in Act 1 on the way Eliza speaks (*A woman who utters such depressing and disgusting sounds*) illustrates his own eloquent speech and his passionate love for language. ❂ Find some other places where Higgins uses language to great effect, perhaps giving little thought to how it affects others.

AN ILL-MANNERED BULLY

Higgins shows lack of politeness to other people and completely disregards conventional manners. His housekeeper comments on his bad language and his appalling table manners. His social behaviour is poor, as shown in the scene with Mrs Higgins's guests, where he uses improper language and is unsuitably outspoken. He is abrupt, off-hand and tactless with everyone; his mother has to point out that he behaves rudely. At the beginning of the experiment Mrs Pearce tells him: *You can't walk over everybody like this* (Act 2).

+ then he changes his tactics → thus he coaxing does try to walk over everyone + get his own way. But is he aware of it?

A LIKEABLE ECCENTRIC

Higgins says in defence of his bad manners that he treats everyone the same – he has *the same manner for all human souls* (Act 5). Higgins cares *for life, for humanity* (Act 5) and he dedicates his life to improving the human race through the application and development of scientific knowledge. His lively and creative mind makes him relish Doolittle's impudent honesty and poetic language. Higgins's zest for life and learning makes him take on the challenge of turning a flower girl into a duchess, and he finally develops enough finer feeling to respond to her soul rather than to her voice or face. Mrs Pearce remains his housekeeper in spite of his poor behaviour, and Pickering also remains loyal, although he can see Higgins's faults. We are told in the Sequel that Eliza is still *immensely interested in him.* ❷ In what ways do you find Higgins appealing, or unappealing?

Eliza Doolittle

'A GOOD GIRL'

Eliza comes from a poor background and has learnt to fend for herself. As soon as she was old enough to earn her own living she was turned out of home by her stepmother (her sixth) and has scraped a living selling flowers on the street. Eliza is independent, with a strong sense of morality. Her respectability and good name are important to her, as she frequently asserts with plaintive cries such as: *I'm a respectable girl* (Act 1) and *I'm a good girl, I am* (Act 2). Eliza's comment to Higgins in Act 5, *I could have been a bad girl if I'd liked,* reminds us that she has chosen not to turn to crime or prostitution and has maintained her good reputation. This illustrates Eliza's strength of character.

DETERMINED TO IMPROVE

Eliza is ambitious and set on improving her position. Her determination to become one of the middle class with a job in a shop makes her approach Higgins for lessons. Eliza shows that she is quick-witted and quick to learn, and both Higgins and Pickering are amazed at her superb memory and her ability to reproduce sounds. In Act 4 and Act 5 we see the transformed Eliza. She has learnt to speak differently, but more than that, she is confident and controlled and can express herself fluently and forcefully. Eliza calls herself a *common ignorant girl* (Act 4). ❂ How do you react to this description?

HURT

Eliza is hurt by Higgins's treatment of her and his indifference to her situation. The comments she makes in Act 4 about her position reveal her sharp intelligence and her wounded feelings, as when she pertinently asks to whom her clothes belong and refers to the next girl they pick up to experiment on. Eliza's hurt feelings and desperation are seen in her cry *What's to become of me?* in Act 4, and her statement in Act 5, *I'm a slave now, for all my fine clothes.* Eliza comments to Higgins that when he feels lonely without her he can listen to her voice on the machine and look at photographs of her. ❂ What might this suggest about Eliza's confidence and self-esteem?

DEVOTED

In spite of her confident exterior, Eliza remains vulnerable. She has become devoted to Higgins and Pickering, and is hurt by Higgins's insensitive comments: *Don't sneer at me. It's mean to sneer at me* (Act 5). Eliza retains a sense of pride and dignity, telling Higgins: *I'm not dirt under your feet.* Finally she stops being afraid of Higgins and asserts her independence. Her decision to marry Freddy shows her need for affection and kindness, and she willingly accepts the responsibilty of looking after and supporting him.

Alfred Doolittle

Doolittle is something of a cheeky rogue. He enjoys his job as a dustman because it easier than working at his real trade, and it keeps him firmly at the bottom of the social and economic ladder. Doolittle does not want any responsibility in life, and in particular he does not want to be burdened with the morality that is attached to being respectable. Doolittle's dislike of responsibility leads him to accept £5 rather than £10 because he cannot drink up the greater sum in a weekend. Doolittle is proud of being one of the Undeserving Poor. His shameless amorality and his eloquent language delight Higgins. ✪ Why is 'Doolittle' an appropriate name for this character?

Doolittle's life is transformed when he becomes wealthy. He has been forced to give lectures on moral reforms, and so must become respectable. Doolittle complains about his new responsibilities, which include getting married and dealing with people who want money from him.

Colonel Pickering

Colonel Pickering is a courteous gentleman with a military background. He is a language scholar who admires Higgins's work so much that he comes to London to meet him. He is kind and gentle to Eliza, treating her with politeness and addressing her as *Miss Doolittle*. His manners contrast with Higgins's lack of courtesy, and Eliza appreciates his gentlemanly treatment of her.

Pickering does try to act as a curb on Higgins, for example in Act 2 when he agrees with Mrs Pearce that Eliza should understand fully what she is taking on. He says that he feels responsible for Eliza, and he does try to protect her from Higgins's extreme behaviour. However, Pickering admires Higgins and shares his enthusiasm for the experiment, even if he does show more consideration than Higgins does for Eliza.

Mrs Higgins

Mrs Higgins is a strong-minded, cultured woman who treats her son with affection and firmness. She is intelligent and sensitive in her dealings with others, as when she sympathizes with Mrs Eynsford Hill's poverty-stricken state, and when she shows concern about Eliza's future. When Eliza leaves Wimpole Street, Mrs Higgins gives her a home. In Act 5 we see her tact as she acts as a go-between for Eliza and Higgins, and when she asks Doolittle to leave the room to give Eliza time to make it up with Higgins and Pickering. Mrs Higgins is open-minded and tolerant, but speaks her mind when it is necessary.

Freddy Eynsford Hill

Freddy is a weak young man, who at the beginning of the play hasn't enough *gumption* to get a cab. He is something of a figure of fun with his affected speech and his ineffectual behaviour. Freddy has no money and has not been brought up to work. He cannot change his expectations because he is poor. Freddy would not lower himself to take a job that he considers to be beneath him. However, although weak and silly, he loves Eliza and gives her the kindness and affection she needs.

Mrs Eynsford Hill

Mrs Eynsford Hill is a poor member of the upper middle class trying to maintain her position in society. Shaw describes her as well bred and quiet. She seems aware that Clara's behaviour is pushy, and explains to Mrs Higgins at the end of their visit to her house that Clara does not get many social opportunities because they are so poor.

Clara Eynsford Hill

Clara appears to Higgins and his mother to be a *disagreeable and ridiculous person* (Afterword). She is snobbish and silly, treating Eliza with disdain when she is a flower girl and hanging on to her every word when she appears to be a fashionable lady. Her desire to be accepted makes her gullible, and she is easily fooled into believing that Eliza's language is the *new small talk*.

Mrs Pearce

Mrs Pearce, Higgins's housekeeper, is loyal to and protective of Higgins. She is not sure whether to admit Eliza into the house, and repeats Higgins's instructions to the girl: *Sit down, girl. Do as you're told* (Act 2). Sometimes Mrs Pearce feels that she needs to excuse Higgins's behaviour, as when she tells Eliza in Act 2: *You don't understand the gentleman*. In spite of her liking for Higgins, Mrs Pearce does comment on his bad table manners and his use of swear words. She is concerned for Eliza and the problems she will face in the future.

Test yourself

? Write down the name of each character. Decide which words from the following list describe which character. Write the words under the name. You can use the same words to describe more than one character.

expert thoughtless loyal obsessed sympathetic ambitious enthusiastic considerate amoral determined unconventional tactless intelligent affectionate respectable confident vulnerable strong-minded weak tactful kind independent irresponsible courteous snobbish protective

? Test yourself by using the Mini Mind Map on p. 13 and the full Mind Map on p. 20, as suggested at the start of the chapter.

Now that you're familiar with this cast of colourful characters, work your way around the Mind Map on the next page, then have a short break before looking at the play's themes.

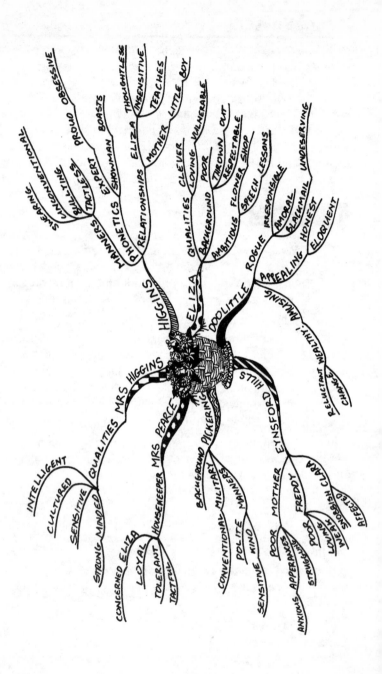

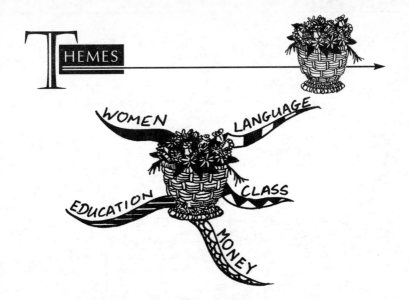

THEMES

A theme is an idea developed or explored throughout a work. The Mini Mind Map above shows the main themes of *Pygmalion*. Test yourself by copying the Mini Mind Map, adding to it, and then comparing your results with the version on p. 27.

Language

Shaw's passionate interest in language is evident throughout *Pygmalion*. The main character in the play is a professor of **phonetics** (the study of the sounds of the spoken language and how they are represented by signs). Shaw campaigned for the introduction of an alphabet which would indicate the sounds of the letters, so that everyone would be able to speak the language more clearly and communication would be more effective. Eliza learns to speak differently by pronouncing words phonetically, according to certain sounds, rather than by pronouncing the letters of words as they appear on the page.
○ Look at Eliza's first speech for an example of a phonetic alphabet.

However, *Pygmalion* is not a play about phonetics; the science of phonetics just provides a basis for the play's ideas about people and their relationships with each other and with society.

It explores a range of aspects of language, such as the connection between the way people speak and their social position. In the first act, Higgins identifies people's backgrounds by their speech. The *depressing and disgusting sounds* (Act 1) of Eliza's accent provide Higgins with the challenge which is the centre of the whole drama. Eliza will learn to disguise her origins by speaking differently. When she adopts a new accent, she is taken as a member of a different class. By showing how society can be fooled in this way, Shaw mocks and attacks the practice of classifying people as worthy or unworthy by their use of language.

Pygmalion illustrates that people's language is no indication of their worth. The most upper-class accent is that of Freddy, who is seen to be weak and silly. The 'lowest' accents are Eliza's and Doolittle's, yet these two characters have colour and vitality in their speech as well as their personalities. Eliza does not become a better person when she learns a different accent, but we see that her accent was, in fact, the only 'low' thing about her. She has learnt the kind of grammar, vocabulary and pronunciation that enable her to move into a different social class, but her moral awareness and the self-respect and independence we see at the end of the play are admirable aspects of her character that are not dependent on the way she speaks. ✪ What can a person's speech reveal? What can it not reveal?

Pygmalion also examines attitudes to bad language, or swearing. Higgins is reprimanded by Mrs Pearce in Act 2: *You swear a good deal too much*, and both Pickering and Mrs Higgins say that his coarse language will be a bad example for Eliza. Higgins is a gentleman, yet he uses improper language. ✪ Why does Higgins use this kind of language? What is Shaw suggesting about his character? What point is being made about middle-class standards of behaviour?

Clara's attitude to language reveals Shaw's dislike of snobbery and pretentiousness. She is ready to copy Eliza's speech because she has been told that it is fashionable. Mrs Eynsford Hill's complaint about young ladies using strong expressions such as *filthy* and *beastly* illustrates the way that conventions of language use change, and also highlights Shaw's dislike of middle-class affectations.

Class

Pygmalion presents a picture of the class system in England at the beginning of the twentieth century. The upper class of rich landowners who lived on inherited wealth and did not have to work are represented in the embassy scene, the middle classes are represented by the Eynsford Hills, the Higgins family and Pickering, and the working classes by the Doolittles. Doolittle places himself in a subdivision, the idle poor.

Shaw's impatience with the class system is seen in the way he challenges the Victorian belief that a person is born into a certain class and should remain in it. He believed that people should not be limited by their birth. Through Eliza he shows that class barriers can be broken down and equality achieved. Eliza wants to become one of the respectable middle classes. Before she even begins her speech lessons, her appearance is changed through the application of soap and water. Here Shaw shows his rejection of the idea of a genuine poor class; the poor are distinguished by their appearance only because they haven't got access to the means of keeping clean. Eliza's triumphant entry into a higher class through changing the way she speaks adds to the suggestion that class differences are to some extent based on superficial factors and the practice of judging people by speech, clothes and appearance rather than by their innate worth.

Doolittle delights in rejecting and mocking the morality of the middle class. He prides himself on being one of the *undeserving poor*, who do not show the virtues, such as thrift and honesty, which encourage the other classes to give them charitable donations. In a comic inversion of conventional attitudes to class, Doolittle does not see his eventual entry into the middle class as a triumph, but as a disaster. In the Afterword we hear that Doolittle rises still further socially and mingles with the aristocracy. Here Shaw mocks the upper class who turn Doolittle into a kind of intellectual hero, just as he mocks the upper class in the scene at the embassy for their silliness and gullibility. Shaw also ridicules some of the attitudes held by the middle and lower classes. ❂ What do you think about the way different classes are presented in *Pygmalion*?

23

Money

Class and money are closely linked in *Pygmalion*. Eliza's poverty is seen in the description of her room, with its broken window pane mended with paper and the wallpaper peeling off the walls because of the damp. Her assertion *I won't be called a baggage when I've offered to pay like any lady* (Act 2) indicates the low expectations of her class. Eliza's statement suggests that respect can be bought and that people without money are not entitled to respect. ❂ What do you think of this idea? What does Shaw think of it?

As a flower girl Eliza earned an honest if meagre living. When she becomes a lady she has to find a different way to support herself because social standards and ideas about class make it unsuitable for a middle-class lady to sell flowers on the street. The Eynsford Hills provide a good example of these attitudes. Although Freddy has no money he will not consider taking a job that he thinks is beneath him, and Mrs Eynsford Hill anxiously struggles to maintain her position in society without making any concessions to her impoverished state.

Doolittle tries to get money from Higgins in exchange for Eliza. He pretends to be concerned for his daughter's virtue but in fact has spotted an opportunity for some lucrative blackmail. When this ruse fails he talks Higgins into parting with five pounds. Eliza says his trade is *talking money out of other people's pockets into his own* (Act 2). However, Doolittle is not out to make as much money as possible. He refuses ten pounds, because such a sum would have to be handled responsibly. He delights in being poor and not bound by the same code of morality as the middle class. When Doolittle comes into a large sum of money he is burdened by the responsibilities it brings, but feels he cannot refuse the money because it brings him a secure future. ❂ Are you surprised that Doolittle accepts the bequest? Remember that Mrs Higgins tells him he can refuse to accept the money. Can you see any difficulties in suddenly becoming wealthy?

Education

Shaw believed that social progress could be made through education, and that an educated population would lead to a better, more equal society. From 1870 basic education was made available to all, and working-class people became more literate and more able and inclined to stand up for their rights. The central concept in *Pygmalion*, Eliza's rise from being seen as a flower girl to being seen as a princess, illustrates Shaw's belief in self-improvement. Eliza takes the opportunity that is available to her and builds on her natural assets, improving her situation in life by means of Higgins's training and her own ability and determination. Neither Freddy nor Clara has had any serious secondary education, but unlike Eliza they do little or nothing to improve themselves. ❂ Do you believe that society can be improved through education? What kind of education? How do you think a more ideal society may be achieved?

Women

Shaw was a staunch supporter of equal rights for women and men. His attitude to the subject of equality is seen in his creation of Eliza, a strong character who retains her independent spirit and can argue effectively with the clever, intimidating Higgins. Mrs Higgins is another example of a strong female character. In some ways she is like Henry, outspoken and forthright and somewhat eccentric. She is more than a match for her son, dealing with his careless manners with wit and humour, and showing an understanding of life and people that is far superior to Henry's. Mrs Higgins and Mrs Pearce immediately see the problems of Eliza's role in the experiment whereas the male characters are slower to grasp the implications.

Higgins does not know how to deal with women. He tells Pickering in Act 2 that he becomes *selfish and tyrannical* when he is friends with a woman, and he comments on the difficulty of a woman wanting to live her own life and a man wanting to live his. He says: *Women upset everything.* ❂ What do you think Henry means by this? His answer is to be a *confirmed bachelor*, in spite of his mother's wish that he would fall in love with a nice-looking young woman (Act 3). ✪ How serious is Henry when he says that his mother is his ideal type of woman? What qualities do you think Henry admires in his mother?

Think about the themes

? Draw each theme icon on a separate sheet of paper. (You could make up your own icons.) Write or draw all the characters who are connected with each theme.

? Test yourself by using the Mini Mind Map and full Mind Map, as suggested at the begining of the chapter.

Now you're clear about the themes, check out the Mind Map on the next page, then take a break before getting in on the acts.

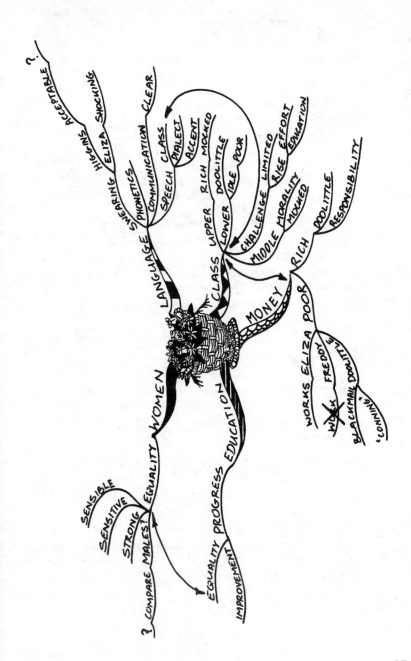

27

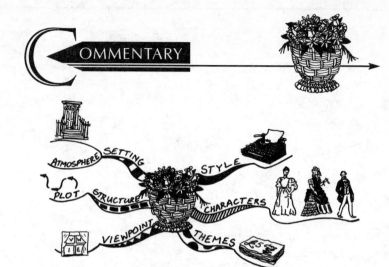

COMMENTARY

The Commentary looks at each scene in turn, beginning with a brief preview which will prepare you for the scene and help in last-minute revision. The Commentary comments on whatever is important in the section, focusing on the areas shown in the Mini Mind Map above.

ICONS

Wherever there is a focus on a particular theme, the icon for that theme appears in the margin (see p. x for key). Look out, too, for the 'Style and language' sections. Being able to comment on style and language will help you to get an 'A' in your exam.

You will learn more from the Commentary if you use it alongside the play itself. Read a section from the play, then the corresponding Commentary section – or the other way round.

QUESTIONS

Remember that when a question appears in the Commentary with a star ✪ in front of it, you should stop and think about it for a moment. And **remember to take a break** after completing each exercise!

Preface to *Pygmalion*

◆ The English alphabet should be replaced by a phonetic alphabet.

◆ Henry Sweet, a language scholar and phonetician, is the basis of Higgins's character.

◆ People can change their accents, and should apply the science of phonetics to help them.

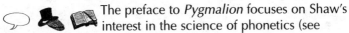 The preface to *Pygmalion* focuses on Shaw's interest in the science of phonetics (see p. 21). Shaw vigorously argues that English spelling has nothing to do with the way words are pronounced and should be reformed through the introduction of a new phonetic alphabet. Class divisions are emphasized by different ways of pronouncing the same word: *it is impossible for an Englishman to open his mouth without making some other Englishman despise him.*

Shaw is delighted that *Pygmalion* is so successful, in spite of dealing with the subject of phonetics and being didactic (intended to teach something). He believes that great art always teaches us something.

Before you go on

? Speak out loud the word *fish*. What sound do you make at the beginning of the word? What letter represents that sound? Now try saying *laugh*. What sound do you make at the end of the word? What letters represent that sound? Think of some more examples of confusing sounds and spellings in English.

? Start a Mind Map of what you think *Pygmalion* teaches us. You could add to it as you work your way through the Commentary.

Sheltering from the rain

Act 1

(To p. 10, *[She retreats in disgust behind the pillar].*)

◆ A group of people shelter from the rain in Covent Garden.
◆ Freddy Eynsford Hill is trying to get a cab for his mother and his sister Clara.
◆ Freddy bumps into Eliza, a flower girl.
◆ Mrs Eynsford Hill is surprised that Eliza seems to know Freddy.
◆ A man (Higgins) is secretly taking notes on what is going on.

The opening scene takes place in London's Covent Garden, an area where middle-class theatre-goers mingled with the workers from the fruit and vegetable market. The Eynsford Hills are established as middle class by the way they speak and by their evening dress. Clara and her mother are critical of Freddy's failure to get them a taxi cab. Clara calls him: *You selfish pig.* Clara is shown to be complaining and self-centred. The rude way she insists that her mother should get the change for the bunch of flowers suggests her lack of real manners and her disdain for people she thinks are beneath her. Her comment *Sixpence thrown away!* indicates that the Eynsford Hills are not well off. Mrs Eynsford Hill is more polite to Eliza, and she tells Clara to be quiet, but this is partly because she wants to find out how Eliza knows Freddy. She is shocked that this low-class flower seller with a Cockney accent should be able to call her son by his first name. However, Mrs Eynsford Hill might as well have saved her money – Eliza calls every stranger either Freddy or Charlie.
❂ How do you respond to the Eynsford Hills? What does Shaw want us to think of them?

Eliza's appearance and speech show that she is poor and uneducated. The stage directions emphasize her lack of cleanliness and her worn, grubby clothes. Eliza speaks good-naturedly to Freddy when he bumps into her, but exclaims about his bad manners when he rushes off after damaging her flowers. She shows spirit in the way she asks Mrs Eynsford Hill to pay for the flowers; we are also made aware of her struggle to earn a living.

STYLE AND LANGUAGE

Notice the way Shaw uses the dramatic device of a heavy shower of rain to bring together a variety of people of different types and from different classes. He needs to present a range of accents so that Higgins can display his brilliance. ❸ How do modern theatre and television dramatists bring together a range of different people?

Shaw uses phonetics to represent Eliza's first speech. Although he reverts to conventional spelling after her first speech, the use of phonetics does give us an idea of how Eliza speaks, and of how tough a job Higgins will face.

The note taker

(From p. 10, *An elderly gentleman ...* to p. 13, *... to interfere with a poor girl.*)

◆ An elderly man (Pickering) joins the sheltering group.
◆ Eliza tries to sell him flowers.
◆ Eliza is warned that Higgins is taking notes.
◆ Higgins imitates Eliza's speech and identifies where Eliza and the rest of the group come from.

Pickering is described as *an amiable* military gentleman. We see his good nature as he looks for some change to buy Eliza's flowers, although her badgering him to buy is *troublesome*. He reassures Eliza that he has no reason to make a charge against her and tells the crowd: *Anybody could see that the girl meant no harm.* He tries to soothe Eliza, telling her that Higgins can't touch her. Higgins's summary of Pickering's life, that he was born in Cheltenham, went to school at Eton and university at Cambridge and served with the army in India, which was part of the British Empire, identifies Pickering as one of the upper middle classes with a conventional education and background.

Eliza's pushy wheedling for small sums of money demonstrates her determination and emphasizes the difficulty of scraping a living. We can assume that Eliza has begun to make a better life for herself; she left her home in Lisson Grove because *it wasn't fit for a pig to live in.*

31

Eliza is determined to keep her good name and shrieks that she is a *respectable girl*. Her wild crying and hysterical protestations of her innocence are comic, but also highlight for us the position of women of Eliza's class. Eliza earns a respectable living and has not fallen into crime or prostitution as a means of supporting herself, but she is aware that a charge of soliciting could be trumped up against her: *They'll take away my character and drive me on the streets for speaking to gentlemen.* The only defence Eliza has is to proclaim her innocence and her respectability in loud and raucous tones, repeating herself with mounting hysteria. Eventually she is reassured that Higgins is not a detective or police informer, and subsides with mutterings that she is a *good girl.*

Higgins brusquely dismisses Eliza's fears, calling her a *silly girl* and telling her to *shut up*. We can see his overwhelming interest in language when he immediately asks for an explanation of the term *copper's nark*. Higgins deals in a friendly way with the crowd's initial antagonism, identifying in turn where the bystanders and Eliza come from. Notice how precisely he can pinpoint people's backgrounds by the way they speak, identifying different areas in London, for example. He becomes the centre of attention and dominates the crowd with talent and his confident manner. Higgins seems to enjoy performing for an audience. He swings the crowd round to his side when he reels off the names of the places where Pickering was born, where he was educated and where he served with the army. ❂ What regional or other types of accent can you identify? Do you classify people by the way that they speak?

The bystanders and the crowd provide further examples of the way people speak. The bystanders use grammatical forms such as *He won't get no cab* and *it ain't my fault*. How do these expressions differ from Standard English? (Standard English is the kind of language you read in most published writing, that you use in most writing you expect somebody else to read, and that you hear in contexts such as news broadcasts, parliamentary debate, business and the law.) The bystanders also add to the picture of the class system as seen in the play. They show solidarity with Eliza when they think that she may be in trouble. Notice that one of them tells her to make sure that she gives a flower to Pickering in return for his coins, to make it clear that she is taking money for flowers and not for sexual services. This bystander classifies Higgins as a gentleman because of his boots, and calls him *sir*. The crowd shows resentment of Higgins at first, suspecting him of being a police spy, and are also suspicious of his insight into their backgrounds. The comment *You take us for dirt under your feet* expresses resentment at the way Higgins assumes the right to expose something of their private lives. However, they enjoy the way Higgins subjects Pickering, another gentleman, to the same treatment.

Check out some characters

?   Who bumps into Eliza and knocks her basket out of her hands?

?   Who complains about Eliza getting sixpence for flowers that are a penny a bunch?

?   Who is taken for a policeman?

?   Who comes from Hoxton?

?   From what you've seen so far, circle in one colour the words below that describe Eliza, in another colour those that describe Higgins, and in a third colour those that describe Pickering. Underline words that apply to more than one character.

educated   determined   polite   spirited
defensive   intelligent   confident
arrogant   outspoken

Take a quick break before a stream of insults and a boast!

'I could pass you off as the Queen of Sheba'

(From p. 14, ... THE DAUGHTER (*out of patience*), to
p. 16, ... *can you believe that?*)

◆ The rain stops and people begin to go home.
◆ Higgins and Pickering discuss language and phonetics.
◆ We learn that Higgins makes a living by teaching people to speak properly.
◆ Eliza continues to moan and complain.
◆ Higgins claims he could pass Eliza off as a duchess.

Clara rudely pushes her way to the front of the crowd and violently turns on Higgins when he murmurs his assessment of her pronunciation. Clara is angry and peevish, saying to Higgins when he offers to get them a cab: *Don't dare speak to me.* Mrs Eynsford Hill is more polite. She is intrigued by Higgins's accurate identification of her background and thanks him for his help.

Higgins says that phonetics is his profession and his hobby. We see that it is a subject that has become an obsession. Ironically, although Higgins prides himself on being able to place within two miles or even two streets where a person comes from, he makes money by teaching people to conceal their real origins. People who become wealthy and wish to climb the social ladder ask Higgins to help them to speak differently. ❂ What do you think about people who want to change the way they speak?

Higgins becomes so irritated with Eliza's self-pitying complaints and snivelling that he explodes at her to *cease this detestable boohooing instantly.* What incenses him is not what Eliza says but the way that she says it. He refers to the *depressing and disgusting* sounds that she makes. He expresses violent anger at the fact that Eliza debases the English language by *crooning like a bilious pigeon.* Higgins is highly insensitive in the venomous way he addresses and treats Eliza. He shows her no respect as a human being, referring to her as *this creature* when he talks to Pickering and alluding to her life *in the gutter.* His insults mount as he calls her a *squashed cabbage leaf* and *an insult to the English language.* ❂ What do you think about the way Higgins speaks to Eliza? Is it funny?

Can you justify it in any way? The insulting and deprecating references to Eliza emphasize Higgins's confidence and arrogance as he claims to be able to change the way Eliza speaks to such an extent that she will be taken for a duchess.

Look at Higgins's comment that a shop assistant requires better English than a duchess. ✪ What does this comment suggest about the upper class or the aristocracy? Later on Eliza says: *I don't want to talk grammar. I want to talk like a lady in a flower shop.* ✪ What do you think she means?

STYLE AND LANGUAGE

Higgins, Pickering and the Eynsford Hills speak the dialect known as Standard English. A dialect is a variety of English that has its own vocabulary and grammatical features. Any dialect may be spoken in any accent, accent being the way we pronounce words. The kind of pronunciation Higgins teaches is the accent known as Received Pronunciation (RP). In the play, this is the accent associated with the high social classes.

Check out some language issues

?   Find three examples of non-Standard English from this section.

?   Try speaking the words in illustration A in Received Pronunciation and the words in illustration B in a Cockney accent..(Look at Eliza's first speech to remind you of the sounds.)

? Write a sentence explaining what Higgins dislikes
about the way Eliza speaks. Write a sentence
explaining how Eliza will have to change the way she
speaks if she is to be taken for a duchess.

*A squashed cabbage leaf into a duchess?
Perhaps going home in a taxi is a start —
have a break before visiting Eliza's room.*

I know you!

(From p. 16, THE GENTLEMAN *Of course I can,* to the end of the Act.)

◆ The two men introduce themselves: Henry Higgins, author
of *Higgins's Universal Alphabet,* and Colonel Pickering,
author of *Spoken Sanskrit.*
◆ They have been keen to meet each other.
◆ Eliza makes a last attempt to sell Pickering flowers.
◆ Higgins throws money into her basket.
◆ Freddy returns with a cab.
◆ Eliza goes home in the cab.

The two men's pleasure and excitement at
discovering each other's identity creates a bond
that emphasizes their academic interests and excludes Eliza.
Eliza tries one more time to get Pickering to buy some flowers,
saying that she needs the money to pay the rent. Higgins
accuses her of lying about this, but then his conscience is stirred
and he casually throws a handful of coins into her basket.

Eliza relishes the opportunity of riding home in style. She
grandly dismisses Freddy, calling him *young man* as she
mimics upper-class behaviour and sweeps into the cab he had
procured for his mother and sister. This humorous display
together with Higgins's ill-mannered treatment of Eliza and
Clara's rudeness to others forms a comment on manners and
the way people treat each other. A confused Freddy is left
raising his hat. ✪ What impression have you gained of Freddy

in this Act? Notice that the taxi driver isn't going to let Eliza into the cab until he sees her money. ❷ As you read the play, consider what is suggested about the power of money and what it can and cannot buy.

The taxi driver seems to enjoy Eliza's play-acting when, for Freddy's benefit, she asks to be taken to Buckingham Palace. He familiarly calls her *Judy*, and a class solidarity is established between them as he comments that Eliza's real destination is a much more likely address for her sort of person. He is amused by her obviously false claim that she is used to travelling in cabs and, admiring her spirit, sportingly lets her off the fare. Eliza, however, finds this humiliating.

The description of Eliza's room shows her ambition and aspirations. The pictures torn from newspapers and pinned on the wall suggest that she dreams of a life beyond her poverty-stricken environment. ❷ What details of the description show how poor she is?

STYLE AND LANGUAGE

The play's structure hinges on four major locations. This Act takes place in Covent Garden, which was both a fashionable meeting place and the home of London's largest fruit and vegetable market. It buzzed with activity throughout the day and night; on chilly mornings, pubs were still open from the night before. Covent Garden provides an ideal setting for diverse characters to meet.

During Oliver Cromwell's rule in the early seventeenth century all theatres were closed. When new theatres were built after 1660 they were sited in the Covent Garden area. *Pygmalion* was first performed in His Majesty's Theatre situated to the west of Covent Garden.

Over to you

? What impression have you gained of Eliza and of Higgins? Begin a Mind Map of their characters to show the important things they do and say and how you respond to them.

? Which is your favourite character so far? Which do you like least? Draw a circle and divide it to show the relative appeal of each character.

? Put these objects in the order in which they appear in this Act.

Now you've reached the end of the first Act, do something different, then go on to see what happens when Eliza arrives at Higgins's laboratory.

The bet

Act 2

(To p. 27, *You can't walk over everybody like this.*)

◆ Higgins shows Pickering his laboratory.
◆ Eliza turns up.
◆ Eliza wants to pay Higgins to teach her to speak.
◆ Pickering challenges Higgins to a bet.
◆ Higgins will pass off Eliza as a duchess in three months' time.

The description of Higgins's laboratory emphasizes the scientific nature of his language experiments. Details such as a *life-size image of half a human head, showing in section the vocal organs* and a *laryngoscope* help to create this impression. The description of this scene in *My Fair Lady*, the musical adaptation of *Pygmalion*, leaves out these particular details. ❂ What reasons can you think of for this? Shaw's description of Higgins points out that he is voraciously interested in anything that can be studied as a scientific subject. This alerts us to the fact that Higgins may well ignore the human element in relationships and may single-mindedly pursue the interests of scientific activity. Look at the rest of the description of Higgins. ❂ What positive aspects of his personality are shown? Higgins's expertise is highlighted by Pickering's comment that he has taken in only half of what Higgins has shown him.

Mrs Pearce, Higgins's housekeeper, identifies Eliza as *common*, and remarks on her dreadful accent. Higgins is delighted with the prospect of an interesting subject for his work; notice that he plans exactly how he will record his visitor's speech before he even knows who she is. This indicates Higgins's eccentricity and total absorption in his work. When Higgins recognizes Eliza he tells her to go – she is no use to him as he has already recorded Lisson Grove speech. Higgins shows no sensitivity towards Eliza, and hardly seems aware that she is a person. He often speaks of her in the third person as if she is not present: *this girl's income; She's so deliciously low*. Higgins's references to Eliza as a *guttersnipe* and a *baggage* and his instructions to Mrs Pearce to *Wrap her up in brown paper* and to wash her with Monkey Brand, a very strong soap that was used to clean kitchen equipment, imply that Eliza is an object, robbed of humanity. Higgins's conversation with Eliza combines mockery, threats, intimidation and total superiority. ○ Can you find an example to illustrate each of these?

Eliza's proposition intrigues Higgins. He works out that proportionately her offer is the biggest he has ever received, and is considering accepting it when Pickering challenges him to teach Eliza to speak like a lady in time for the ambassador's garden party. Higgins embraces the challenge with gusto; his interest is aroused and he is quickly carried away with the excitement of the idea. He sees Eliza as the subject of a fascinating experiment. ○ What do you think of Higgins's attitude?

Eliza's appearance shows that she is trying to make a good impression. She has tried to clean and tidy her clothes, and flaunts three brightly coloured ostrich feathers in her hat. ○ What effect does Eliza mean to create with the feathers? What effect is created? Eliza speaks to Higgins with spirit and confidence. She tells him not to be so saucy, and clearly thinks that he should show her some respect because she has arrived in a taxi and can afford to pay for lessons. We see Eliza's drive and ambition as she plans to move towards an independent livelihood in a flower shop. Eliza has already begun to climb the social ladder, having moved from Lisson Grove to Drury Lane, and is now taking steps towards securing the respectability and status of a shop job. ○ What do you think of Eliza's decision to ask Higgins to teach her? What does this decision and the process by which she may have arrived at the decision tell you about Eliza's character?

In this scene Eliza shows a mixture of pride, dignity, bewilderment and insecurity. She gives a pathetic display of dignity when she makes it clear that she can afford to make Higgins this business proposition. She is confident enough to tell Higgins that a gentleman would ask her to sit down, but squeals in humiliation when Higgins calls her a *baggage* and jokes about throwing her out of the window. Notice that Eliza feels that since she can pay, she shouldn't be treated like dirt.

❂ What do you think about this point of view? She recovers her poise sufficiently to suggest with jaunty confidentiality that Higgins might have been drinking the night before, when he threw the money to her, but her confidence is pricked once more as both Higgins and Mrs Pearce speak sharply to her. Eliza feels on safer ground when discussing the amount she is willing to pay, having worked out how much lessons in speaking English should be worth, and being determined not to be cheated. However, she cannot understand Higgins's assessment of what proportion of her income a shilling represents and dissolves into tears. The contrast between what a shilling means to Eliza and what it means to Higgins and Pickering is both humorous and pointed, highlighting the economic division between the classes.

Eliza is offended by the comment that she is dirty, and by Higgins's instruction that her clothes should be removed. Her assertion *I'm a good girl, I am* and her threat to call the police show Eliza's outraged respectability and her instinct for self-protection. Her suspicions that she is in danger of being seduced (and later, drugged) is amusing and at the same time draws attention to the precarious position of women who do not have the protection of money or education. Higgins's reproof of Eliza: *We want none of your Lisson Grove prudery here* indicates different class attitudes to matters concerning the body. His comment suggests that Eliza's lower-class background has caused what he regards as a false sense of shame.

Colonel Pickering is gentle and courteous towards Eliza. His invitation to her to sit down is more polite than Higgins's or Mrs Pearce's, and he supports Eliza's declaration that she should keep the handkerchief that Higgins gives her. He shows dry humour when he comments that Higgins is not going to turn Eliza's head with flattery. However, it is Pickering who comes up with the idea of the bet: *I'll bet you all the expenses of the experiment you can't do it*. Pickering also joins in with Higgins's teasing recital of a piece of verse based on Eliza's name. ❂ Which do you think is stronger, Pickering's admiration of Higgins or his instinct to be kind to Eliza?

From the beginning Mrs Pearce is uneasy about Eliza's role in Higgins's household. She is protective and proud of her

41

employer, making the most of opportunities to remind Eliza that Higgins is a gentleman and that she is just a *poor ignorant girl*. Mrs Pearce has misgivings about Higgins's plan and hopes that Pickering won't encourage him *to do anything foolish*. She speaks firmly to Higgins, telling him to be reasonable and pointing out that he is behaving in a bullying way: *You can't walk over everybody like this*.

Try this

? Eliza wants to improve her situation in life. Choose from the list the factors that could be most helpful to her. Put them on the rungs of the ladder, the most important at the top.

speaking differently   fashionable clothes
intelligence   money   confidence
copying the way other people speak   education
a rich man   determination   motivation   self-respect

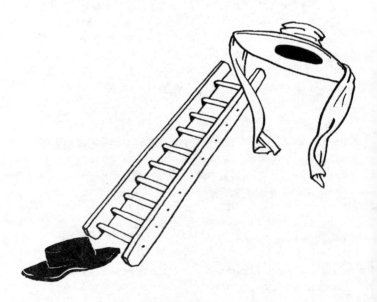

? What do you imagine the flower-shop owner thought of Eliza? Fill in the thought bubble.

The experiment takes shape

(From p. 27, *[Higgins, thus scolded , subsides ...]* to p. 32, *[Eliza's plaints are no longer audible].*)

◆ Mrs Pearce foresees problems.
◆ Colonel Pickering sees the need for caution.
◆ Higgins persuades Eliza to be the subject of the experiment.

Mrs Pearce has several objections to Higgins's plan. She points out that Higgins knows nothing of Eliza's background. When Higgins calls Eliza a wicked girl, Mrs Pearce tells him that he is the wicked one, and advises Eliza to go back to her parents. Mrs Pearce senses some potential danger to Eliza, although it is not the same kind of danger that Eliza suspects. She wants to know the terms and conditions of

Eliza's stay in the household. ✪ Why does Mrs Pearce dislike Higgins's plan? Most significant is Mrs Pearce's warning to Higgins that he should look ahead and think about what will happen to Eliza when the experiment is over. Mrs Pearce shows a greater sense of responsibility than Higgins, and her fears for Eliza's future anticipate what happens later in the play when Eliza herself accuses Higgins of callous disregard for her position. In the end Mrs Pearce reluctantly accepts the situation. Her comment to Higgins that he never thinks or cares what may happen to people illustrates her sense of morality and Higgins's thoughtless selfishness. ✪ What do you think of the relationship between Higgins and his housekeeper?

Colonel Pickering is less outspoken than Mrs Pearce, but he feels that he must voice his misgivings. He thinks it important that Eliza should understand what she is letting herself in for, and points out to Higgins that Eliza has feelings. However, he does so in a good-humoured way rather than a forceful way and although he tries not be sidetracked by Higgins's dazzling rhetoric – *Very clever, Higgins, but not to the present point* – his objections are swept aside. ✪ Is there any way that Pickering could stop Higgins going ahead with the experiment? Do you think he wants to?

Higgins employs a range of techniques to ensure that he gets what he wants. He speaks soothingly to Mrs Pearce and Colonel Pickering saying that they must all be kind to Eliza and help her to prepare for her new station in life. He uses *thrillingly beautiful low tones* to convince Eliza that after his teaching she will be irresistible to men, then abruptly reverts to brusqueness when she is unimpressed, telling Mrs Pearce to *Throw her out* and calling Eliza an *ungrateful wicked girl*. He speaks of Eliza with great insensitivity. He says that she is of no use to anyone except him and dismisses the idea of paying Eliza because she would only spend the money on drink. ✪ Do you think that he means everything he says? Higgins's comment that we can *throw her back into the gutter* when the experiment is over shows his lack of moral responsibility. At the beginning of this Act, Shaw says that *Higgins remains likeable even in his most unreasonable moments*. ✪ How could an actor make Higgins likeable in this scene?

Higgins's obsession with his own interests is amusingly illustrated when Eliza tells him that she has feelings, and for a moment Higgins reflects on this *difficulty*. However, it is not the difficult issue of Eliza's sensitivities that occupies him. He has listened not to what Eliza says, but to the way that she says it, and is struck by how difficult it will be to teach Eliza to speak grammatically. This difficulty becomes the focal point for comedy later on, when Eliza has learnt how to pronounce words in the required accent, but has not learnt the grammar and vocabulary of her new dialect.

Higgins tempts Eliza with chocolate and the promise of countless rides in taxis. He piles on references to gold and diamonds, and spins a fantasy about Eliza's marriage to an officer in the Guards. Higgins is carried away by his delight in using language and playing with ideas. In the speech beginning *That's all you'll get out of Eliza*, Higgins gives Eliza instructions, bribes and threats, some wild and ridiculous and some that will strike a chord with Eliza. ❂ Do you think Eliza believes that her head will be cut off if the King finds out that she is not a lady? What about the promise that she will sleep in a proper bedroom? Decide which suggestions are possible and which are fantasy.

Eliza reveals that her father and stepmother turned her out of home to earn her own living. ❂ What do you think of the way Eliza has gone about supporting herself? She declares herself unimpressed by Higgins's ideas, saying that he's *off his chump*, but is easily cowed by his threats to throw her out. We see Eliza's pride when she declares that she can buy her own clothes, and in the way that she insists on her good name being respected. Once more we hear her refrain *I'm a good girl*, and her respectability is shown in her resentment of the suggestion that she drinks. Eliza stands up to Higgins. She tells him that he should be ashamed of himself and that she is going, but she is tempted by what Higgins offers. Eliza is confused and bewildered. However, she defiantly tells Higgins that he's a bully and declares that she won't stay if she doesn't want to and that no-one is going to be allowed to wallop her. Eliza clings on to her belief in her own honesty and integrity, and her belief in her right to her feelings. Although she is reluctant and suspicious, Eliza stays and follows Mrs Pearce to the bathroom. ❂ What advice would you give Eliza at this point in the play?

Try this

? Put these lines of dialogue in the order in which they appear.

You shall have a present of seven-and-sixpence to start life with as a lady in a shop.

Does it occur to you, Higgins, that the girl has some feelings?

This is the young woman, sir.

You don't understand the gentleman.

I'll take her anywhere and pass her off as anything.

I haven't taken in half of it, you know.

Take all her clothes off and burn them.

? How does Mrs Pearce treat Eliza? How does she treat Higgins? Make a Mind Map of your ideas.

Eliza's bath

(From p. 32, *[Eliza is taken upstairs ...]* to p. 35, *[Eliza's screams are heart rending]*)

◆ Mrs Pearce takes Eliza upstairs to give her a bath.
◆ We discover that Eliza has never had a bath before.
◆ Eliza is reluctant to undress and get into the bath.

This scene adds to the play's humour through its observation of manners and customs, and also makes us aware of the different ways of life experienced by the different classes. Eliza has never seen a bath before and the prospect of climbing into it and getting wet all over fills her with horror. Her knowing reference to a woman who died from having a weekly bath shows the lack of education typical of Eliza's class. Eliza also reveals that she has never taken off all her clothes before. Look at the reasons she gives for sleeping in her clothes. ❂ How do Eliza's explanations affect your view of her and people like her? How does the audience react to Eliza's screams at the end of the scene? Mark the places in the scene where you think an audience would laugh.

Higgins's habits

(From p. 35, *[Meanwhile the Colonel ...]* to p. 39, *[She admits Doolittle and retires.]*)

◆ Colonel Pickering is concerned for Eliza.
◆ Mrs Pearce asks Higgins to be careful how he behaves in front of Eliza.

Pickering questions Higgins about his relationships with women. He feels some responsibility for Eliza and wants to be assured that Higgins won't take advantage of her. Pickering shows concern for Eliza's welfare and the morality of the experiment.

Higgins says that he is a *confirmed old bachelor* because he finds it difficult to deal with women, and becomes selfish and tyrannical the moment he becomes friends with a woman. He claims that even his best-looking pupils could be blocks of wood as far as he is concerned. ❖ Is Pickering right to be concerned? What do you think of Higgins's view of his relationships with women? Is it true that he is unfeeling towards his female pupils? Is it true in the way that Higgins means it? Higgins refers to himself as a *shy, diffident sort of man*, and says he cannot understand how Mrs Pearce can think that he's an *overbearing, bossing kind of person*. ❖ How much self-knowledge does Higgins possess? Shaw tells us that Higgins can behave with *stormy petulance*. ❖ Can you find an example of such behaviour in this section?

Mrs Pearce expresses concern about Eliza's language. Notice that she doesn't repeat the word *bloody*; such a word would not be acceptable in polite society. However, she points out that Higgins uses this word indiscriminately and should not let Eliza hear him. Higgins cleverly brushes aside Mrs Pearce's observation by saying that he was just using **alliteration** (the repetition of a sound at the beginnings of words), but Mrs Pearce is not sidetracked by his frivolity. She reminds him of his slovenly dress and habits, his untidiness

47

and his poor table manners. ✪ How do you react to this insight into Higgins's behaviour? How important are social manners?

Notice that Pickering fears that they will have some trouble from Eliza's father, but Higgins is only interested in his accent.

Enter Doolittle

(From p. 39, [*Alfred Doolittle is an elderly* ... to p. 46, *Beg pardon, miss.*)

◆ Doolittle tries to blackmail Higgins.
◆ Higgins threatens to call the police.
◆ Doolittle backs off and settles for £5.
◆ On his way out Doolittle meets Eliza.

We are told that Doolittle is an *elderly but vigorous* dustman. ✪ How do you think he should speak and move throughout this scene? Why is he shown to be wearing his dustman's clothes? We are prepared to meet an angry father anxious for his daughter's welfare, but instead we see a *blackguard* out to make some money. Doolittle's plan is to blackmail Higgins by pretending to want Eliza back at home, so that Higgins will pay to be 'allowed' to keep her living in his household. When Higgins calls his bluff by saying he can have Eliza, Doolittle protests and wheedles: *Don't take a man up like that, Governor.*

Doolittle talks his way into Higgins's favour. He puts on a musical and melancholy voice and launches into the story about how he knew where to find his daughter. Doolittle projects a range of roles as he gives his account. His remark that the public house is the *poor man's club* shows him to be a cynical social observer and spokesman for the working class, while his reference to *my feelings and my duty as a father* shows that he wants to be seen as a conscientious and dutiful parent while in reality he is selfish and manipulative. Doolittle attempts to reinforce the image of himself as a good father when he puts on a mock-honest tone and asks Higgins what, as a parent, he was supposed to think about Eliza not wanting her clothes sent on. When he realizes that he is not fooling Higgins with his show of moral righteousness he tries to establish fellow feeling between them: *You and me is men of the world, ain't we?* ✪ How does Shaw want audiences to react to Doolittle?

Finally Doolittle tells the truth and comes out with his proposition, which he presents as if he is doing Higgins a favour. He says that Eliza is a *fine handsome girl*, but *not worth her keep* as a daughter. ✪ What do you think about the way he refers to Eliza, and about the way he tries to sell her off for £5? Doolittle says that if he thought that Higgins had sexual designs on Eliza he would have asked £50. ✪ How do you react to this? What do you think about Doolittle's morality?

Doolittle says that he can't afford to have morals. He classes himself as one of the *undeserving poor*. He is referring to the tradition by which charity goes to poor people who are perceived to be deserving – this means that they behave in a way of which *middle-class morality* can approve. They are seen to live blameless lives, and will spend charitable donations sensibly and prudently. Doolittle argues eloquently for people like him who don't deserve anything but who still have needs. He is amusing and honest about what he needs. He needs to eat, and he drinks a lot more than a 'deserving' man. He needs money to cheer him up when he's down. If Higgins gives him a fiver he will spend it immediately on a drunken weekend spree with his *missus*. As Doolittle sees it, he has a right to do this and he shouldn't be denied his pleasure by middle-class ideas about how others should behave. ✪ Does Doolittle have a point? Would you give him money? Doolittle won't take more than £5 because that sum is just enough to splurge without beginning to feel prudent or responsible. He likes being one of the *undeserving poor* and being able to live in a free and easy way without responsibility. ✪ What other 'responsibility' has Doolittle avoided so far?

Higgins is intrigued and delighted by Doolittle. At first he adopts a bullying manner to his visitor and makes it clear that Doolittle is not going to get away with blackmailing him. Then Higgins is impressed by Doolittle's rhetorical and picturesque speech. He likes the rhythm of Doolittle's words: *I'm willing to*

tell you. I'm wanting to tell you. I'm waiting to tell you.
Higgins recognizes that Doolittle is dishonest and a liar, but
says it is accounted for by his Welsh ancestry. Pickering's mild
reproof of Higgins's sweeping generalization adds to the
amusement of Shaw's dig.

Higgins is most impressed by Doolittle's speech about the
Undeserving Poor. He thinks that Doolittle has shown such skill
with words and such boldness in argument that, with some
coaching in how to speak, he could be a preacher or a Member
of Parliament. ✪ What does this suggest about what Shaw thinks
of the institutions of the Church and of government?

Eliza's first lesson

(From p. 46, THE JAPANESE LADY ... to the end of the Act.)

◆ Doolittle doesn't recognize Eliza at first.
◆ Eliza never wants to see Doolittle again.
◆ Eliza's new clothes arrive.
◆ Eliza has her first elocution lesson.

Eliza is freshly bathed and wearing one of the Japanese
garments that Higgins brought back with him. Doolittle's
comments that he never thought she could look so good and
Eliza's observation *Now I know why ladies is so clean* suggest
that the difference between the classes is superficial. We see
the friction between the father and daughter. Doolittle does not
seem to realize the contradiction when he says first that Eliza
is a credit to him, and then that he never brought her up at all.
He speaks in a heavy-handed way to Eliza, assuming the right
to tell her how to behave towards Higgins and telling him how
to treat Eliza: *If you want Eliza's mind improved, Governor,
you do it yourself with a strap.*

Eliza thinks it is a disgrace that Doolittle works as a dust
collector instead of at his real trade. The difference between
Doolittle and Eliza is that Eliza wants to escape from her class
and become one of the middle classes that her father mocks.
Eliza wants to take a taxi to her old corner to show her old
friends that she has risen in the world. Higgins warns her
against snobbery. ✪ Do you think Eliza could become a snob?
Do you agree with Higgins's definition of the word?

Shaw tells us that when Eliza is waiting for her first lesson she feels like a hospital out-patient meeting her doctors. ✪ What does this comparison suggest? If it were not for Pickering's reassuring presence, Eliza would have run away. ✪ What is Eliza feeling at this point?

 Higgins is outraged by the way Eliza pronounces the language of Shakespeare and Milton. He refers to Eliza as an *unfortunate animal*. Even when he is pleased with her progress he refers to her in the third person: *By Jupiter, she's done it at the first shot*. Higgins threatens that he will drag Eliza around the room by her hair (like a 'cave man') if she goes back to her old way of speaking, and offers chocolate to stop her crying. ✪ What do you think of Higgins's teaching methods? Are they successful?

STYLE AND LANGUAGE

The location of this Act is Higgins's laboratory in Wimpole Street. Wimpole Street was an area associated with the professional middle classes. Shaw wants the laboratory to suggest a positive view of the new science of phonetics, to reflect his belief that an academic can be a hero with the power to change the world by changing the way people speak. An early film version of *Pygmalion* showed the laboratory to be like a torture chamber and the experiment to be a rather sinister type of social engineering. ✪ What do you think about the nature of Higgins's experiment? How important is the laboratory location?

Over to you

？   Draw a circle around the words that describe Doolittle:
       scheming   hardworking   clever   stupid
       honourable   weak   determined   responsible
       lovablelazy   hypocritical   honest   amoral
       eloquent   inarticulate   sensitive

？   Who speaks these lines:

       I want to change you from a frowzy slut to a clean respectable girl.

What is middle-class morality?

He'd as soon you set a bulldog on him as a clergyman.

You are doing very well; and the lessons won't hurt.

? Imagine that Mrs Pearce is telling a friend about Eliza's bath and Doolittle's arrival. Write some notes about what she would say. You could record your ideas in a Mind Map.

? Make a Mini Mind Map of Higgins's teaching methods. You could then make a Mini Mind Map of your own thougths about ideal teaching methods, and a Mini Mind Map showing the differences between the two.

Has the experiment worked? Take a break before Eliza makes her first entrance into middle-class society.

Mother and son

Act 3

(To p. 54, *[... but before he reaches it his mother introduces him]*)

◆ Mrs Higgins is expecting guests.
◆ Henry Higgins bursts in.
◆ He has invited Eliza to his mother's tea-party.

The description of Mrs Higgins suggests that she is strong and independent. We are told that she *defied fashion in her youth* and that now she is *long past taking the trouble to dress out of the fashion.* The paintings and objects in Mrs Higgins's room indicate that she has cultured and artistic tastes.

Mrs Higgins is outspoken. She makes it clear that she is dismayed by Henry's arrival because he has promised not to visit on her 'at-home' days. His manners and conversation offend her friends and drive them away. Mrs Higgins is firm with Henry, insisting that he must leave. She is witty and clever: when Henry says that he has no *small talk* (an expression that means light conversation) she points out that it is his *large talk* (an expression she invents) that upsets people. Mrs Higgins speaks to Henry as if he is a small boy. She tells him to stop fidgeting and to take his hands out of his pockets.
❂ Are Mrs Higgins and Henry at all similar?

Although Mrs Higgins is firm with her son and embarrassed by the way he treats her guests, she is very fond of him and is concerned for his welfare. She would like him to fall in love with a young woman. However, she is neither predictable nor conventional. When Henry says that he supposes she wants him to marry, her definite *No* is amusing and indicative of her character. Mrs Higgins shows good humour and tolerance in her attitude to life and in her treatment of her son.

Higgins makes it clear that a few months have passed and that Eliza's pronunciation has changed. He wants his mother to notice not just how Eliza speaks, but also what she says. Mrs Higgins's observation that the subject of health may not be a safe one prepares us for what happens later, and shows that she is more perceptive than Henry. We see Henry's admiration for his mother when he says: *My idea of a lovable woman is somebody as like you as possible.* His single-mindedness can be seen in the way he bursts in and insists on using her tea-party as a testing ground for Eliza.

The Eynsford Hills again

(From p. 54, *Mrs and Miss Eynsford Hill* ... to p.57, ... *to indicate to her which lady is her hostess.*)

◆ Mrs Eynsford Hill and Clara arrive.
◆ Colonel Pickering and Freddy arrive.

Shaw tells us that the Eynsford Hills are part of an upper class, but do not have any money. Perhaps because of their impoverished state, Clara in particular is very eager to be part of society. Henry's behaviour towards the Eynsford Hills shows his abrupt manners and lack of polite speech and gestures. He bluntly indicates that he can remember their accents but not their faces. Mrs Higgins has to apologize for her son. ❂ According to convention, how should Henry behave? What mistakes does he make? Mrs Higgins has to remonstrate again with Higgins when he says *damn it* to Colonel Pickering. Another example of his thoughtless rudeness is when he tells the Eynsford Hills that he needs two or three people and they will do as well as anybody else.

With Freddy's arrival, the scene is set for Eliza's entrance. Higgins is bored and impatient. His continued use of expressions such as *what the devil* and his inability to make polite conversation illustrate his disregard for conventional behaviour. Clara tries to establish fellow-feeling with Higgins, seeing him as potential husband material, but her comment that she hasn't any small talk and that she wishes people would say what they think plunges Higgins into gloom. ❂ Does Clara really wish that people would say what they think? What function do you think 'small talk' fulfils? What kinds of subject are considered to be suitable for small talk, and what kinds of subject are considered to be unsuitable?

Eliza at the tea-party

(From p. 57, [Eliza, who is exquisitely dressed ...] to p. 60, [She goes out])

◆ Eliza's impressive entrance.
◆ Eliza pronounces her words carefully and correctly.
◆ The inappropriate subject matter and vocabulary of Eliza's conversation.

Eliza's appearance creates an impression of *remarkable distinction and beauty*. She has been groomed in dress and deportment and seems to be a self-possessed member of society. The Eynsford Hills have no idea that she is the flower girl they met in the first act, although Mrs Eynsford Hill feels that Eliza's eyes seem familiar.

Eliza is on safe ground as she carefully repeats the phrase *How do you do*, remembering to pronounce the H in *How*. She has been instructed to restrict her conversation to the subjects of the weather and health. Eliza, therefore, picks up Mrs Higgins's opening conversational question about the likelihood of rain, and launches into a beautifully pronounced weather forecast. Eliza doesn't realize that she is using vocabulary and a style of speech which are inappropriate for a conversation. ✪ What kind of response would Eliza have been expected to make? She is proud of her performance, so she rounds on Freddy when he laughs. Freddy thinks this is all part of Eliza's up-to-the-minute fashionable way of speaking.

When Mrs Eynsford Hill mentions influenza, Eliza spots another conversational opening. Unfortunately she discusses the circumstances of her aunt's death, including dark hints that her aunt had been killed, and an account of how Doolittle ladled gin down her throat. Not only is the subject matter lurid and inappropriate for polite society, but Eliza also uses slang expressions and grammatical constructions that are out of place in the kind of English she is trying to speak. Eliza says *she come through influenza* instead of *she came*, and says *Them she lived with* instead of *Those she lived with*. Slang expressions Eliza uses include *done her in* and *pinched*. The reference to the straw hat that Eliza hoped to inherit adds to the contrast between Eliza's appearance and accent and what she says. The humour comes from this contrast between Eliza's perfect pronunciation and the content and style of her speech, and also from the fact that Eliza is not aware of the effect of her conversation. ✪ How do you respond to Eliza at this point? Why does Higgins choose his mother's tea-party for Eliza's first public outing in her new role?

Eliza is encouraged by the attention of her listeners and confidently continues her account of her father's alcohol consumption. She observes that he was always better-tempered when he'd had a drink, and with an air of wisdom and confidentiality adds that many women have to make their husbands drunk to make them fit to live with. When Eliza realizes that Freddy is laughing, she asks Higgins: *Have I said anything I oughtn't?* Notice that it is Mrs Higgins who reassures Eliza. ✪ Why does Mrs Higgins do this? At this point, Higgins gives Eliza a hint that she should leave. ✪ What do you think he is feeling at this moment?

Eliza says her goodbyes with dignity and impeccable pronunciation. She is almost safely out of the door when, in response to Freddy's query if she is going to walk across the park, Eliza with *perfectly elegant diction* replies *Walk! Not bloody likely*. Her use of the word *bloody* shocks her listeners. However, Eliza does not realize the sensation she has caused and sweeps out of the room.

 ### STYLE AND LANGUAGE

The publicity caused by Eliza's use of the swear word increased the play's popularity. The press loved it because it gave them an opportunity for some eye-catching headlines: 'Mrs Patrick Campbell [the actress playing Eliza] had to use a word which the *Daily Sketch* cannot print.' The Daily Sketch also reported that the audience laughed so much at this point that the play stopped for a whole minute. Audiences also loved to hear the infamous word spoken by the actress Mrs Patrick Campbell, who usually played roles exhibiting proper drawing-room behaviour. ❂ What do you think about Shaw's use of the word? What effect does he want to create?

Over to you

?   Who –
- likes getting pretty postcards in shorthand?
- is told to stop fidgeting?
- ladled gin down someone's throat?
- admires *the new small talk?*
- sees no indication of any great change in the barometrical situation?

?   If you were directing the play, how would you want Higgins, Mrs Higgins, Pickering and the Eynsford Hills to look and behave during Eliza's visit? Write a note for each actor about how he or she should react.

?   In *My Fair Lady*, this scene is set at the Ascot Races instead of at Mrs Higgins's tea-party. Can you think of any reasons for this?

'The new small talk!'

(From p. 60, *[Pickering gasps and sits down]*, to p. 62, *[She goes out]*)

- Clara thinks she has discovered a fashionable new way of speaking.
- Mrs Eynsford Hill does not like the new 'small talk'.
- Freddy is interested in Eliza.

Clara's desire to be fashionable means that she is easily fooled. She believes that Eliza's inappropriate vocabulary is an up-to-date way of speaking. Clara says that such language is *quaint, delightful* and *innocent,* and that any objection to it is just Victorian prudery. Higgins teases her by suggesting that she should try out the new language at the three visits the Eynsford Hills are going on to make. ✪ What kind of reaction is Clara likely to get if she follows his suggestion? What do you think of Higgins's trick? Clara delightedly uses the word *bloody* as she leaves, convinced that she is demonstrating how fashionable she is.

Pickering is kind towards Mrs Eynsford Hill. He understands her dislike of some of the changes in the kind of language used in polite society, and reassures her that she need not use the word *bloody.*

Mrs Higgins is also kind and sensitive in this scene. She listens sympathetically when Mrs Eynsford Hill explains that they are very poor and that Clara has little experience of society. Notice too that Mrs Higgins has observed Freddy's fascination with Eliza, and invites him to visit again.

STYLE AND LANGUAGE

Shaw's portrayal of Clara illustrates some of his ideas about language. He disliked the practice of upper-class people adopting working-class slang expressions, just as he disliked people with no knowledge of phonetics trying to imitate upper-class speech. As Shaw says in the Preface to *Pygmalion,* an *honest slum accent* is preferable to poor attempts to mimic the language of the upper classes. Eliza's natural way of speaking is vigorous and compelling, with far more life than

the kind of drawing room conversation she aspires to. In this scene Eliza gets it wrong, but her character and her use of language have an appeal and authenticity that contrast with Clara's silly affectedness.

Freddy tries to imitate upper-class speech, for example with his greeting *Ahdedo*. ❍ What is Freddy saying? Speak the word out loud.

Mrs Higgins is worried about Eliza

(From p. 62, HIGGINS (*eagerly*): *Well?...* to p. 66, *Oh, men! men!! men!!!*)

◆ Mrs Higgins asks about Eliza's position in the household.
◆ Mrs Higgins asks what will happen to Eliza when the experiment is over.

Mrs Higgins points out that Eliza has not changed sufficiently to be taken as a member of society. Every sentence she speaks reveals her social origins. Mrs Higgins refers to Eliza as a triumph of art – the new Eliza has been created through the skills of Higgins and of her dressmaker – but she will not be a perfect creation unless she learns a different mode of speech. Higgins's own language is not a good example.

STYLE AND LANGUAGE

Mrs Higgins's comments remind us of the statue made by Pygmalion in the Greek myth. Higgins's remark: *you have no idea how frightfully interesting it is to take a human being and to change her into a quite different human being* is another reminder of the myth. Higgins is an artist 'creating' Eliza just as Pygmalion sculpted the statue which came to life as a beautiful woman. Pygmalion fell in love with his statue, Galatea. ❍ Do you think that the audience expects Higgins to fall in love with Eliza? Do you think that Higgins does fall in love with Eliza?

 Mrs Higgins is firm with Henry, who stops talking at a word or a touch from his mother. Mrs Higgins is also firm in the way she pursues the subject of

Eliza's position in the household, showing a concern that is understood by Pickering, at least. She is sharp and critical of the two men, commenting that they are like babies playing with a live doll. Mrs Higgins's intelligence and perception make her question what will become of Eliza afterwards. She does not agree that Eliza has been given *advantages* by Henry. She says that Eliza is being turned into a fine lady, but does not have an income to support a fine lady's way of life. We see Mrs Higgins's exasperation with the two men at the end of the scene when she rises with *an impatient bounce* and *grips the table angrily*. Mrs Higgins, unlike Henry, sees Eliza as a real human being who will have to get on with her own life once the experiment is over. ✪ Which other character shares Mrs Higgins's worries about Eliza? Mrs Higgins calls Henry and Pickering *two infinitely stupid male creatures*. ✪ What do you think of this comment?

Higgins exhibits a range of behaviour typical of his excitable, contradictory character. He is offended by the reminder that he uses strong language, then sulkily accepts the truth of the comment. Higgins is excited by the successful start to his scheme, and cannot see Eliza as anything but the subject of his experiment: *It's the most absorbing experiment I ever tackled.* He doesn't understand Mrs Higgins's concern for Eliza's unclear status in the household. ✪ What worries Mrs Higgins about Eliza's living in Henry's house? Do you think she is right to be worried? Higgins casually reveals that Eliza is useful to him in matters such as remembering his appointments, and defensively points out how hard he has to work to change her speech. He dismisses his mother's warnings about Eliza's future with the careless comment: *We'll find her some light employment*, and dismisses Mrs Pearce's constant reproofs that he doesn't think about what he's doing with Eliza as *some silly bee in her bonnet*. Higgins is totally absorbed in accomplishing his own aims.

Pickering is also absorbed in the experiment, as we see when he and Higgins excitedly talk at the same time, getting louder and louder until they are shouting at each other. Pickering, though, is the first to apologize for the noise, showing the considerate nature he also displays when he tries to reassure Mrs Higgins that he and Higgins will do what's right for Eliza. Higgins exclaims about Eliza's parrot-like ability to mimic any sound she hears, and Pickering praises Eliza's ability to hear music at concerts and play whatever she hears on the piano. Both men are amused and entertained by her gift for mimicry. However, Eliza's exceptional gift for mimicry enables her to learn and shows her to be a gifted intelligence. (Mimicry is a good way to learn. Try it yourself – for example with writing styles.) ✪ How does Pickering treat Eliza? Is his treatment of her different from Higgins's or Doolittle's?

STYLE AND LANGUAGE

Mrs Higgins's flat is another of the play's major locations. The flat is situated in Chelsea, an area with artistic and bohemian associations, and the style of decoration indicates Mrs Higgins's sympathy with the pre-Raphaelite movement in art and her sense of beauty. Shaw places Mrs Higgins in a setting that reflects *her cultivated sense of the best art of her time* (Afterword, p. 106). Try to see a stage or film version of *My Fair Lady*. You will notice that in these versions Mrs Higgins is placed in a different setting, and that she appears as a more conventional motherly figure. ✪ What kind of person do you think Mrs Higgins should appear to be?

The embassy

(From p. 66, *Clearly Eliza will not pass as a duchess yet*, to the end of the Act.)

◆ Eliza attends the reception at the embassy.
◆ An expert in languages is present.
◆ Eliza is taken for a Hungarian princess.
◆ Higgins has won his bet.

Eliza's appearance arouses great interest and tension builds as we wait to see if her behaviour and conversation have changed sufficiently to allow her to carry off the deception. The character of Nepommuck, an ex-pupil of Higgins who is present as an interpreter, adds to the tension with his claim to be able to *place any man in Europe*. Nepommuck's intention to blackmail the Greek diplomat who is trying to hide his origins heightens the challenge that faces Eliza.

This is the moment that Eliza used to dream about. She passes through the reception like a sleepwalker, every nerve strained with the effort of concentration. The effect she creates is so stunning that people stand on chairs to see her more clearly. Notice that the only words that we actually hear Eliza speak are *How do you do?* ❂ Why do you think Shaw decided to have Eliza's conversation reported rather than shown? At the end of the scene Eliza thinks she has been unsuccessful, and Pickering has to tell her that she has won the bet ten times over. ❂ What do you think about her comment: *nothing can make me the same as these people?* Is she right? Is this a good thing or a bad thing?

Nepommuck and the people at the reception are presented as objects of ridicule. Nepommuck's claim to be Higgins's *best and greatest pupil* and his pleasure in being known as *Hairy Faced Dick* show his absurd self-importance. The interpreter does realize that Eliza is not what she seems, and his observation that she speaks English as if it were a foreign language is accurate, but his conclusion that Eliza is a Hungarian princess makes it clear that he is no rival to Higgins. He sticks to his theory even when Higgins reveals the truth about Eliza's background. Here Shaw mocks the gullible people who prefer to believe a ridiculous idea than to admit that they have been fooled by an *ordinary London girl out of the gutter.*

Higgins is contemptuous of the people at the reception. His comment that the hostess must find this sort of thing a *fearful bore* shows his impatience with the conventions of polite society. Higgins dislikes the pretentiousness and lack of intelligence of this social group: *I have had enough of chattering to these fools.*

STYLE AND LANGUAGE

The embassy is the fourth important location. As with the other locations, it is associated with particular types of accents and attitudes. The formal background of the reception provides a suitable testing ground for Eliza's performance.

A workout for your memory muscles

?   What might the people at the embassy reception say about Eliza? Write one or two sentences.

?   Circle the words in the list below that apply to Higgins. Circle in another colour the words that describe Mrs Higgins. Underline any words that apply to both.

    thoughtful   mischief-making   intelligent   tolerant   sensitive   selfish   outspoken   petulant   critical   exasperated   imaginative   perceptive   polite   well-spoken   elegant   persistent   knowledgeable

?   Write a sentence describing Freddy's thoughts as he leaves the tea-party.

?   How can you use the technique of mimicry to help your learning? Make a Mini Mind Map of your ideas. (You could think about how you 'become' a character, and how you 'mimic' effective writing styles.)

?   What might happen when Clara tries out the *new small talk* with her mother's friends? You could write a short piece of dialogue, or if you are working with friends, have some fun and act it out!

That's the end of Act 3. Eliza has been a great success — so why isn't she pleased and happy? Find out after the break.

Eliza is ignored

Act 4

(To p. 74, *[He goes out.]*)

◆ Higgins and Pickering discuss the successful result of the experiment.

◆ Eliza is upset.

Eliza, Pickering and Higgins have returned to Wimpole Street. Pickering shows consideration for Mrs Pearce, suggesting that they could let her go to bed and that they should tidy up the drawing room. Pickering has enjoyed the day, in spite of feeling nervous about the outcome of the experiment, and he praises Eliza generously for her great success. He is full of admiration for her professional performance. However, notice that Pickering, like Higgins, talks about Eliza and not to her. Pickering makes it clear that Eliza has also been on display at a garden party and a dinner party, before the embassy reception.

Higgins says that he became bored with the experiment as soon as he realized it was going to work. He is more occupied with his thoughts about his dislike of fashionable society – *What a crew! What silly tomfoolery! damned fool of a fashionable woman* – than about what Eliza has experienced. Higgins does not notice Eliza's response and in fact seems unaware of her presence, not even realizing that she brings him his slippers. Higgins only words to Eliza in this scene are casual domestic instructions.

In contrast to the two men, Eliza is *brooding and silent*. We feel her anger mounting throughout the scene. Eliza *flinches violently* when Higgins says he's pleased that the experiment is over, and she looks *murderous* when he says that at last he doesn't need to dread the next day. ✪ What is Eliza thinking and feeling throughout his scene?

Face to face

(From p. 74, *[Eliza tries to control herself ...]* to p. 80, *[...goes upstairs in a tearing rage.]*)

◆ Eliza accuses Higgins of not caring what will happen to her.
◆ Eliza and Higgins quarrel.

Eliza's anger and frustration are seen as she throws Higgins's slippers at him. ✪ What did Eliza do with Higgins's slippers in the previous scene? Shaw uses the image of a trained dog fetching its master's slippers to illustrate the relationship between Higgins and Eliza. When Eliza throws the slippers it is as if she is rebelling against her role as Higgins's 'puppy'.

Eliza's language and behaviour are forceful and vehement. She calls Higgins a *selfish brute* and tries to scratch his face. ✪ Why is Eliza so furious?

Eliza is seriously concerned about her future. The arrangement with Higgins has meant that she has been removed from her old way of life, yet is not part of the life he has introduced her to. Eliza has no means to support herself in her new role. She faces a real dilemma. ✪ Who has already predicted this situation? Eliza scornfully rejects Higgins's suggestion that she should marry *some chap or other who would do very well*. She observes that as a flower seller she didn't have to sell herself, but now as a lady she cannot sell flowers and can only sell herself. Eliza shows pride and dignity, and her intelligence is seen both in her awareness of her situation and in the quality of her argument.

Eliza's query about who her clothes belong to and her request that Higgins should take the hired jewellery for safe keeping show her independence and her awareness of the necessity for self-protection. She also wants to hurt Higgins in retaliation for her own hurt feelings, and once she has succeeded in making him angry, she pushes home the advantage she has gained. Her final way of getting her own back is to return a ring that Higgins bought her, and her cry *Don't you hit me* is calculated to offend Higgins. ✪ How do you think Eliza should say that phrase? How do you think an audience should react? Eliza is delighted when Higgins says that she has wounded him to the heart. She has taunted him to the point where he loses his temper, and she enjoys piercing his confident veneer. Eliza herself maintains her confident pose, *pertly* reminding him to leave a note for Mrs Pearce, until Higgins leaves the room, then she searches for the ring that he threw into the fireplace. Finally Eliza flings down the ring. ✪ What do you think this gesture means?

Higgins is astonished when Eliza throws his slippers at him, and he is amazed and annoyed when Eliza says that she has won his bet for him. Higgins is so absorbed in his own work that he does not appreciate the part played by Eliza in the success of his experiment. He speaks of her in the third person: *The creature is nervous, after all.* ❖ What is the effect of the word *creature*? What similar word has Higgins just used about Eliza? Notice that even when Eliza emotionally accuses him of not caring about her, Higgins's first response is to correct her grammar.

Higgins genuinely does not understand Eliza's distress. He attributes it to the strain of the day and offers her a glass of champagne. When he finally understands that Eliza is worried about her future he is still dismissive of her feelings. Higgins seems to give more attention to the apple he selects to eat than he gives to the question of Eliza's future. He does not see that his two suggestions, that Eliza could get married or that Colonel Pickering could set her up in a flower shop, are offensive to Eliza's self-respect. Should they be? Higgins begins to react only when Eliza refers to *the next girl you pick up to experiment on.* The ideas that he might accuse Eliza of stealing or that he might hit her anger and offend him. Higgins shows real emotion at the end of the scene, and expresses regret that he has wasted his *hard-earned knowledge* on a *heartless guttersnipe.* ❖ Why does Higgins think that Eliza is *heartless*? Do you sympathize with him/her/both/neither in this scene?

Eliza and Freddy

(From *[The furniture of Eliza's room ...]* to the end of the Act.)

◆ Eliza leaves Higgins's house.
◆ She meets Freddy.
◆ Eliza and Freddy drive around all night.
◆ Eliza decides to ask Mrs Higgins for advice.

Freddy is in love with Eliza, and spends his nights gazing up at her window. Eliza is touched and comforted by his affection, and they kiss and embrace. ❖ Why do you think that Shaw describes the couple being moved on, twice, by police constables? How does the first constable respond to Freddy's explanation that he and Eliza have just become engaged?

Eliza says that she was about to jump in the river. ❖ Do you believe her? Has Freddy saved her, by showing her that she is loved and valued? Notice that Eliza is more wordly wise than Freddy, and that she takes the intitiative at the end of the scene. She shows her independence by leaving Wimpole Street. ✪ What do you think of Freddy? Does he have more positive than negative characteristics?

Time to recap

? Have another look at the scene between Eliza and Higgins. Mark where an audience might feel like (a) gasping (b) cheering (c) booing. Mark with a ? any places where reaction might be mixed.

? Which of these men would make the best husband for Eliza? Circle your answer.
- Henry Higgins
- Colonel Pickering
- Freddy
- the cab driver in Act 1
- none of these.
Explain your choice.

? Imagine that you are making a trailer advertising a television production of *Pygmalion*. Choose five pieces of dialogue from the first four Acts to include in your programme. Compare your choices with a friend's.

After Eliza's exit from Wimpole Street, take a break before Doolittle makes a dramatic entry!

A middle-class man!

Act 5

(To p. 91, *[He disappears through the window.]*)

◆ Higgins bursts into his mother's flat.
◆ Higgins and Pickering are looking for Eliza.
◆ Doolittle arrives, dressed as a gentleman.
◆ Doolittle has been forced to become respectable.

Higgins cannot believe that Eliza would have left his house of her own accord. He and Colonel Pickering assume that something must have happened to Eliza, and in their anxiety to find her they inform the police that she is missing. ✪ What reasons does Higgins give for needing to find Eliza?

Higgins is amused when he hears Doolittle's account of how he is now paid to lecture on moral reforms, as a result of being mentioned in a letter Higgins wrote to a wealthy American. As a joke, Higgins had called Doolittle *the most original moralist at present in England.* ✪ Can you remember what Doolittle said on their first meeting to make Higgins refer to him like this? Higgins claims his 'right' to Eliza, saying that Doolittle should not support his daughter as he took £5 in exchange for her. ✪ Is Higgins being serious?

Higgins insists that it was Eliza who treated him badly, and Mrs Higgins will not ask Eliza to come downstairs until Higgins promises to behave. Higgins's sarcasm as he refers to putting on best Sunday manners for *this creature that we have picked out of the mud* shows that he is too self-centred to alter his attitude to Eliza and see things from her point of view.

Doolittle makes a dramatic entrance, elegantly and formally dressed, a very different figure from the dustman we met in Act 2. ✪ How do you think an audience will react when Doolittle appears? Doolittle seems dissatisfied with his new clothes and appearance, and blames Higgins for the change. The humour comes from Doolittle's gloomy preoccupation with his new position in society and his reluctance to accept what would generally be considered as good fortune, and from Higgins's preoccupation with Eliza. Doolittle does not notice that Mrs Higgins is present, and Higgins does not seem to realize the change in Doolittle's appearance. ✪ What does Doolittle mean when he says that Eliza will find him soon enough now? How do you think he should speak this line?

Doolittle has been left £3,000 a year on the condition that he lectures on moral reform. He speaks scornfully of this arrangement, referring to the *blooming will, the blasted three thousand a year*, and the *old blighter* who bequeathed him the money. Doolittle complains bitterly about his new situation, which has forced him to become respectable and middle class. In his long speech on pp. 87–8, Doolitle gives his reasons for not wanting to be a gentleman. He used to be free to behave as he pleased, but now he has to behave in the way that society expects a gentleman to behave. He used to get money out of people (remember the way he got money from Higgins?) and now that he is rich, people are after him for money. Doolittle sarcastically comments that suddenly he has about 50 relatives, all of them poor. We also see sarcasm in his remarks that when he was poor he received free medical treatment and was pushed out of hospital hardly able to stand on his own two feet; now that he can pay for treatment, medical attention is lavished on him. ✪ Does Doolittle have a valid point? Can you see any disadvantages in coming into money? Doolittle predicts that he may have to pay Higgins to teach him to speak properly. ✪ Do you think that Doolittle should change the way he speaks?

As Mrs Higgins points out, Doolittle could refuse to accept the money and the conditions of the will. However, Doolittle cannot reject such a large sum of money. As one of the *undeserving poor* he has not practised thrift, and so the money will rescue him from a penniless old age in the workhouse. Doolittle ends his speech with a dramatic show of emotion as he imagines himself envying the dustmen who empty his rubbish. ✪ Do you feel sorry for Doolittle here?

Mrs Higgins is critical of her son's treatment of Eliza. She points out that Henry must have frightened the girl, and she is annoyed that Henry has given Eliza's name to the police as if she were a *thief, or a lost umbrella*. We see Mrs Higgins's sensitivity and intelligence when she points out that Eliza has become attached to Higgins and Pickering, and how hurt and angry she must be because they have never thanked or praised her. Mrs Higgins's comment that she would have thrown more than his slippers at Henry heightens our sympathy for Eliza.

 STYLE AND LANGUAGE

Doolittle's language is colourful and lively. ✪ What does the **metaphor** in *Tied me up and delivered me into the hands of middle-class morality* suggest about the way Doolittle sees his position? (A metaphor is a description of a thing as if it were something different but also in some way similar.)

Look at the names Shaw uses in connection with Doolittle's transformation. The wealthy American is *Ezra D. Wannafeller*, who is rich through his *Pre-digested Cheese Trust*. Shaw uses humour to make serious points about people and the way they behave.

I'm getting married in the morning

(From p. 91, *[The parlourmaid answers the bell]*, to p. 97, *[... gets his back to the door before she reaches it.]*)

◆ Eliza joins the group.
◆ Eliza compares Higgins's bad manners with Pickering's courtesy.
◆ Doolittle is getting married.
◆ Mrs Higgins and Pickering leave for the wedding.

Eliza speaks and behaves in a confident and dignified way. She ignores Higgins's insults and addresses her remarks to Colonel Pickering. Eliza points out that she has learnt self-respect from Pickering, because he has always treated her with respect: *the difference between a lady and a flower girl is not how she behaves, but how she's treated*. Higgins has taught her grammar and pronunciation, but he has not set her an example of good manners. Higgins's rudeness, swearing and lack of self-control show his contempt for other people. Eliza's claim that she could not sound like her old self is humorously proved false when she catches sight of Doolittle at the window and screeches as she used to.

❂ What do you think about Eliza's ideas? Do you agree that Pickering has taught her more than Higgins?

Higgins is taken aback by Eliza's behaviour. He immediately tries to assert his rights over her by saying that he has put every idea into her head and every word into her mouth.
❂ Is this true? Higgins refers to Eliza as a *thing* he created from the *squashed cabbage leaves of Covent Garden*. ❂ When did Higgins first refer to Eliza as a *squashed cabbage leaf*? How has Eliza changed since then? Higgins arrogantly declares that Eliza will be back in the gutter without him at her elbow.
❂ Is there any truth in what he says?

Pickering's gentle good manners are evident in this scene. He tries to defend Higgins against his mother's and Eliza's criticisms, and is touched by Eliza's thanks. Pickering is quite disturbed by Eliza's reference to the *experiment*. ❂ Why does Pickering dislike the use of this word? Pickering tries to coax Eliza into forgiving Higgins and returning to Wimpole Street.

Doolittle reveals that he is not married to Eliza's mother but that, as a victim of middle-class morality, he is going to marry his present 'wife'. This is the final stage in Doolittle's becoming respectable. He will now live according to the *middle-class way*, a member of the class he used to ridicule.
❂ Do you think that Shaw supports the conventions of middle-class behaviour? Give your reasons.

The final show-down – Eliza and Higgins

(From p. 97, HIGGINS *Well, Eliza,* ... to p. 105, *[... as the play ends.]*)

◆ Higgins wants Eliza to come back, but he won't change.
◆ Higgins likes Eliza's independence, and will miss her.
◆ Eliza is confused about her future.
◆ She decides to marry Freddy and become a teacher of phonetics.

Higgins says that he will not change his manners, and that he treats everybody the same way. ❂ Do you think that this is true? He says that although he can do without Eliza, he will miss her. However, he doesn't want Eliza to wait on him like a servant. He likes her independence and spirit, and doesn't want her to try to buy his affection through looking after him. Higgins wants Eliza back in Wimpole Street for *good fellowship* and for *the fun of it.* ❂ Do you think that Higgins will ever accept Eliza as an equal? Do you think he wants her back because he loves her and is trying to conceal it under bravado?

Higgins doesn't like the fact the Freddy is romantically interested in Eliza and that Eliza may be more interested in pursuing this possibility than in marrying Pickering or allowing Higgins to adopt her. Higgins dismisses Eliza's desire for kindness and affection. He thinks that she is a fool for rejecting what he has to offer, and suggests that her feelings are sentimental and will condemn her to a life in the gutter. When Eliza finally declares that she will marry Freddy and earn an income for both of them through teaching phonetics, Higgins is enraged. At the same time, however, he is full of admiration and sees her as a *tower of strength*. In spite of Eliza's plans for her future, he assumes that Eliza will return to Wimpole Street on equal terms with himself and Pickering, *three old bachelors together*. As Eliza leaves for her father's wedding, Higgins gives her some errands to do on the way home. ❂ Why is Higgins amused that Eliza is going to marry Freddy? Is he really amused? Is he trying to conceal his deep feelings?

In this scene we see Eliza as the finished creation. She has gone further than Higgins had intended;

71

not only can she speak differently, but she emerges as an independent, intelligent woman who is in many ways superior to her creator. We admire the strength of character with which she stands up to Higgins, and her determination to be independent. Eliza's vulnerability as she says she wants some kindness makes the audience warm to her, and we understand her decision to marry Freddy. In a reversal of the traditional male and female roles, she will earn money to support Freddy.
✪ What do you think about Eliza marrying Freddy?

Once Eliza has announced her decision she seems to become more confident. She is no longer frightened of Higgins, and neatly puts him in the wrong by defying him to hit her. Eliza feels she is as good as Higgins, if not better than him, because she can be *kind and civil to people*. Eliza will no longer be cowed by Higgins. She states that she will never see him again, and her final words indicate that she will indeed be a great loss to him, but he will have to do without her.

STYLE AND LANGUAGE

In the myth of Pygmalion, the artist married his beautiful statue. The ending of Shaw's version of the myth is far less romantic – and much more interesting! Higgins accepts at the very end of the play that his creation is an independent being who does not need him. Eliza finds happiness in the kind of warm companionship she would never have with Higgins.
✪ Do you think the play's audiences are likely to feel 'cheated' of a more traditional happy ending? Do you think that Eliza and Higgins are suited to each other? How would you have ended the play?

Over to you

? Which character do you think sings these songs from *My Fair Lady*?
- A song in which someone walks along the street where his loved-one lives.
- A song in which someone longs for a warm and cosy room.
- A song in which someone wants to get to the church on time.

- A song in which someone asks why the English can't teach their children to speak.

? Divide up a circle into a pie to show which character has changed most by the end of the play.

? For each character, think about the type of actor who would be good in the role. Write a brief description of the kind of physical and personal qualities you would look for.

? How similar are Higgins and Doolittle? Make a Mind Map of your ideas.

What happened next

(From p. 105, *The rest of the story* ... to p. 110, ... *contributing to Eliza's support*.)

◆ Shaw explains why Eliza and Higgins don't get married.
◆ Eliza marries Freddy.
◆ Doolittle rises to the top of the social ladder.

Shaw wrote the afterword or sequel to make it quite clear that there is no romantic pairing of Eliza and Higgins at the end of the play. The play is a romance (a story of far-fetched and unrealistic occurrences) because it describes events that are unlikely to happen. Shaw makes it clear that the other meaning of romance (a love story) does not apply to *Pygmalion*. ✪ Why do you think that Shaw found it necessary to point this out?

Eliza is young, intelligent and independent and can choose whom she marries. Her instinct tells her that if she marries Higgins she will constantly be fighting his intimidating superiority and his bullying ways. Furthermore, Eliza recognizes that no woman will rival Mrs Higgins, and that Henry's interest in language will always come first. Henry remains *one of the strongest personal interests in her life*, but he is not a suitable husband for Eliza.

Freddy has no money and no job. ✪ Why does Eliza marry him? Mrs Eynsford Hill cannot help them financially, and Doolittle spends all his money keeping up his new lifestyle. Doolittle has risen higher than the middle class he despises and is now very popular in aristocratic circles.

73

Colonel Pickering to the rescue

(From p. 110, *Thus Freddy and Eliza*, ... to the end.)

♦ Colonel Pickering sets up Eliza and Freddy in a flower shop.
♦ Clara starts work in a furniture shop.
♦ Colonel Pickering has to keep paying bills for Eliza and Freddy.
♦ Eliza and Freddy eventually learn how to run a business.
♦ The shop is finally a success.

Higgins's only comment about the flower-shop plan is that Freddy will make an *ideal errand boy*. ✪ Why is Higgins so contemptuous of Freddy?

Shaw's account of Clara's career highlights the snobbery and inadequacies of the middle class. This class thought itself superior to those who worked in trades such as shopkeeping, and Freddy's family would disapprove of his new venture. However, Clara herself begins to make new friends of an intellectual and literary nature and her snobbery vanishes. Shaw continues to be hard on Clara, though. He describes her as coming under the influence of a novelist, H.G. Wells, with whom Shaw violently disagreed on political matters. Shaw takes this opportunity to mock the novelist and to mock Clara's devotion to him. Shaw describes Clara as an *ignorant, incompetent, pretentious, unwelcome, penniless, useless little snob*. ✪ Does this come across in the play? What does the description of Clara reveal about Shaw and his prejudices?

Eliza and Freddy have no business sense, but through such measures as attending night school and employing other people they eventually make the shop a success. Notice that Shaw avoids a neat happy ending. The shop is not an instant success. ✪ Why does Shaw make this choice? Freddy and Eliza have to become educated in how to run a business, and Colonel Pickering supports them with advice and financial help.

Eliza still finds Higgins fascinating, but she stands up to him now and stops him ridiculing Freddy. She likes Freddy and Pickering, and does not like Higgins. In the end, her 'creator', like Pygmalion, is too godlike for their relationship to be an easy one. Shaw's final words reinforce the idea that his *Pygmalion* is not a romantic love story.

Your final thoughts

? Are you surprised by anything that happens in the Afterword?

? What would happen in your own sequel to the play? Make a Mind Map of your ideas.

? Which of the play's characters would you choose to be stranded with on a desert island? Who would be your last choice?

Well done — you've reached the end of the Commentary. You've earned a break.

TOPICS FOR DISCUSSION AND BRAINSTORMING

One of the best ways to revise is with one or more friends. Even if you're with someone who hardly knows the text you are studying, you'll find that having to explain things to your friend will help you to organize your own thoughts and memorize key points. If you're with someone who has studied the text, you'll find that the things you can't remember are different from the things your friend can't remember – so you'll be able to help each other.

Discussion will also help you to develop interesting new ideas that perhaps neither of you would have had alone. Use a **brainstorming** approach to tackle any of the topics listed below. Allow yourself to share whatever ideas come into your head – however silly they seem. They will get you thinking creatively.

Whether alone or with a friend, use Mind Mapping (see p. vii) to help you brainstorm and organize your ideas. If with a friend, use a large sheet of paper and coloured pens.

TOPICS

1 What does Doolittle add to *Pygmalion*? What would be the effect if his character were to be removed from the play?
2 Which character is most concerned for Eliza's welfare? Give your reasons.
3 What is your reaction to Shaw's determination that Higgins and Eliza should not get married?
4 Choose two scenes, or parts of scenes, and explain how you would present them on the stage.
5 Which character in *Pygmalion* do you most admire? Which character do you admire the least?
6 Discuss the humour in *Pygmalion*.
7 Who do you think has taught Eliza more, Pickering or Higgins?

HOW TO GET AN 'A' IN ENGLISH LITERATURE

In all your study, in coursework, and in exams, be aware of the following:

- **Characterization** – the characters and how we know about them (e.g. what they say and do, how the author describes them), their relationships, and how they develop.
- **Plot and structure** – what happens and how it is organized into parts or episodes.
- **Setting and atmosphere** – the changing scene and how it reflects the story (e.g. a rugged landscape and storm reflecting a character's emotional difficulties).
- **Style and language** – the author's choice of words, and literary devices such as imagery, and how these reflect the mood.
- **Viewpoint** – how the story is told (e.g. through an imaginary narrator, or in the third person but through the eyes of one character – 'She was furious – how dare he!').
- **Social and historical context** – influences on the author (see 'Background' in this guide).

Develop your ability to:

- Relate **detail** to **broader content, meaning and style**.
- Show understanding of the author's **intentions, technique and meaning** (brief and appropriate comparisons with other works by the same author will gain marks).
- Give **personal response and interpretation**, backed up by **examples** and short **quotations**.
- **Evaluate** the author's achievement (how far does the author succeed and why?)

THE EXAM ESSAY

You will probably have about an hour for one essay. It is worth spending about 10 minutes planning it. An excellent way to do this is in the three stages below.

1 **Mind Map** your ideas, without worrying about their order yet.
2 **Order** the relevant ideas (the ones that really relate to the question) by numbering them in the order in which you will write the essay.
3 **Gather** your evidence and short quotes.

You could remember this as the **MOG** technique.

Then write the essay, allowing five minutes at the end for checking relevance, and spelling, grammar and punctuation. **Stick to the question**, and always **back up** your points with evidence in the form of examples and short quotations. Note: you can use '. . .' for unimportant words missed out in a quotation.

Model answer and plan

The next (and final) section consists of a model answer to an exam question on *Pygmalion*, together with the Mind Map and essay plan used to write it. Don't be put off if you don't think you could write an essay as good as this one yet. You'll develop your skills if you work at them. Even if you're reading this the night before the exam, you can easily memorize the MOG technique in order to do your personal best.

The model answer and plan are good examples to follow, but don't learn them by heart. It's better to pay close attention to the wording of the question you choose to answer in the exam, and allow Mind Mapping to help you to think creatively.

Before reading the answer, you might like to do a plan of your own to compare with the example. The numbered points, with comments at the end, show why it's a good answer.

MODEL ANSWER AND ESSAY PLAN

QUESTION

Discuss how Eliza changes in the course of *Pygmalion*.

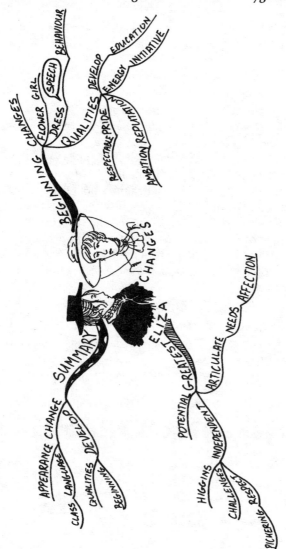

ELIZA CHANGES

BEGINNING CHANGES
- FLOWER GIRL
- SPEECH
- BEHAVIOUR
- DRESS
- QUALITIES DEVELOP
  - EDUCATION
  - ENERGY
  - INITIATIVE
- RESPECTABLE PRIDE
  - AMBITION
  - REPUTATION

POTENTIAL GREATEST
- ARTICULATE
  - NEEDS AFFECTION
- INDEPENDENT
  - HIGGINS
  - CHALLENGES
  - PICKERING
  - RESPECT

SUMMARY
- APPEARANCE CHANGE
- CLASS LANGUAGE
- QUALITIES DEVELOP
- BEGINNING

79

PLAN

1 External and internal changes.
2 Beginning – appearance/speech (change) – energy (doesn't change).
3 Pride, independence, morality (don't change).
4 Ambitious but ignorant – learns – successful change.
5 Potential developed – self-respect – knows what's important.
6 Can articulate needs.
7 Changed externally – inner qualities developed through education.

ESSAY

The most obvious change[1] in Eliza is in her progression from the flower girl in Act 1 to the poised and well-spoken lady we see in Acts 4 and 5. The change is evident in external factors such as Eliza's dress and behaviour, particularly in the way she speaks. To a certain extent the outward change in Eliza is accompanied by changes to her character. However, it is also true to say that in some ways Eliza does not change,[2] that some of the personal qualities which she displays from the beginning emerge most strongly when she has been through a process of growth and education. Shaw's portrayal of Eliza demonstrates his passionate belief in the power of education to enable people to break through the barriers of their birth and environment.[3]

In Act 1, Eliza's appearance indicates her poor background. She is shoddily dressed and grubby, with dirty hair and bad teeth. Her London dialect is strong and she speaks in loud and raucous tones, trying to sell her flowers to the public. She pesters Colonel Pickering so much that he asks her not to be 'troublesome'. The energy that Eliza puts into her flower selling is seen later when she applies herself to Higgins's lessons in how to speak and behave, showing not a change but a development in her character.[4]

Eliza shows pride and concern for her reputation when she complains about Higgins's note-taking: 'He's no right to take away my character. My character is the same to me as any lady's.' In Act 5 she tells Higgins: 'I could have been a bad girl if I'd liked.' Eliza's independence and personal morality have led her to make an honest living and she fiercely protects her good name. Her protestations in Act 1 – 'I'm a respectable girl; I'm a good girl' – are amusing,[5] but her bitter reminder towards the end of the play that as a flower girl she didn't sell herself but as a lady she only has herself to sell makes a serious point about her future. Here Eliza exhibits the same concerns as in Act 1, although her mode of expression is very different.[6]

Eliza's ambition is apparent from the beginning of the play. She has already moved from Lisson Grove to a better environment, and is determined to get a job in a shop. However, her appearance, her uncouth behaviour and her ignorance of such things as baths stand in her way. The first significant change in Eliza's appearance comes when her father does not recognize her once she is clean and dressed in new clothes, and this is followed by her successful appearance at Mrs Higgins's flat, where only the nature of her conversation threatens to reveal her background. With further tutoring, Eliza is a great success at the embassy, where she is taken for a princess. At this point the change in Eliza is seen at its most dramatic.

The greatest change in Eliza, however, is not in the way she dresses and speaks. Her potential has been developed, so that she can assert her indepence in a way that she could not have done at the beginning of the play, first by leaving Wimpole Street and then by standing up to Higgins: 'I'm not afraid of you, and can do without you.' Eliza argues intelligently with Higgins, and shows an awareness of her situation, as when she says, 'I'm a slave now, for all my fine clothes'. Eliza recognizes what began her 'real education' and 'the beginning of self-respect'. When Pickering called her 'Miss Doolittle' on her arrival at Wimpole Street, and continued to treat her with respect, Eliza started to respect herself. Eliza can now understand and articulate ideas about the way people treat each other.[7] Her comment that 'the difference between a lady and a flower girl is not how she behaves but how she is treated' indicates that Eliza can proclaim her own set of values, and at this point I feel that the accent in which she presents her thoughts hardly matters.[8]

Eliza can also articulate her needs. Her decision to marry Freddy shows her desire for affection, which she explains simply: 'Freddy loves me: that makes him king enough for me'. Eliza's determination to work and to support Freddy financially shows the drive and self-reliance she has shown throughout the play. This reversal of the traditional male and female roles may reflect Shaw's support of equality between the sexes. Furthermore, in his refusal to give audiences a romantic happy ending by marrying Eliza and Higgins, Shaw stresses Eliza's independence and her ability to identify her own needs, so creating a strong heroine for an era in which women were fighting for the vote.[9]

We do see a changed Eliza at the end of the play. Her language, appearance and behaviour are different, and she has learnt to deliver what is expected of a woman of the class to which she has risen. Many of the qualities she displays, such as self-reliance, ambition and honesty, can be seen in Eliza the flower girl, but through training and education, not all of it Higgins's, these qualities emerge in a more forceful and focused way.[10]

WHAT'S SO GOOD ABOUT IT?

1 Focuses on question.
2 Establishes an argument.
3 Awareness of context.
4 Sustains argument.
5 Effective use of quotation.
6 Neat ending to paragraph.
7 Perceptive awareness of character development.
8 Personal response.
9 Awareness of social and literary context.
10 Clear, relevant conclusion.

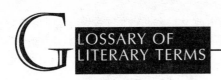
GLOSSARY OF LITERARY TERMS

alliteration repetition of a sound at the beginnings of words; e.g. *depressing and disgusting.*

context the social and historical influences on the author.

dramatic irony where the audience knows something not known by one or more characters.

foreshadowing an indirect warning of things to come, often through imagery.

image a word picture used to make an idea come alive; e.g. a metaphor, simile, or personification (see separate entries).

imagery the kind of word picture used to make an idea come alive.

irony (1) where the author or a character says the opposite of what he or she really thinks, or pretends ignorance of the true facts, usually for the sake of humour or ridicule; (2) where events turn out in what seems a particularly inappropriate way, as if mocking human effort. (See also **dramatic irony**.)

metaphor a description of a thing as if it were something essentially different but also in some way similar; e.g. Higgins calls Eliza a *squashed cabbage leaf.*

personification a description of a thing as if it were a person; e.g. when Higgins calls Eliza *an insult to the English language*, this suggests that English is a person.

phonetics the study of the sounds of the spoken language and how they are represented by signs.

prose language in which, unlike verse, there is no set number of syllables in a line, and no rhyming. *Pygmalion* is written in prose.

setting the place in which the action occurs, usually affecting the atmosphere; e.g. Higgins's laboratory.

simile a comparison of two things different in most ways but somehow similar; e.g. Higgins accuses Eliza of *crooning like a bilious pigeon.*

structure the overall pattern of the plot.

theme an idea explored by an author; e.g. language.

viewpoint how the story is told; e.g. through action, or in discussion between characters.

INDEX

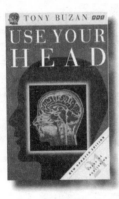